P9-BIL-633

Every Good Desire

ERNEST C. WILSON

G.K.HALL &CO.

Boston, Massachusetts

1974

Library of Congress Cataloging in Publication Data

Wilson, Ernest Charles, 1896-
   Every good desire.

   Large print ed.
   1. Unity School of Christianity — Doctrinal and controversial works.
I. Title.
[BX9890.U5W553 1974]   230'.9'9   74-4356
ISBN 0-8161-6217-4

Published in Large Print by arrangement with Harper & Row, Publishers, Inc.

Set in Photon 18 pt. Crown.

Contents

Preface

"You can if you want to enough!"

This was the challenging assertion that was to change my whole attitude toward life, and launch me on an incredible career.

I am glad that I didn't know how much "enough" meant, or I would have been defeated before I ever got started; but my very limitations served a useful purpose.

When I would be faced with some problem, some challenge, even a great opportunity, often it would seem too much for me. Then I would think, "After all the efforts I've made, all the overcomings, 'Is this the thing that is going to get me down?' and I'd answer myself, 'No, I cannot allow it. I have too much effort invested!'"

And somehow, by the grace of God, with the help of prayer, the subconscious, and the remembrance of past problems overcome, I'd keep on trying, and either the good I sought, or something unexpected and even better than I'd thought, would come to my rescue.

I believe that there is a great, and often undiscovered, potential for successful attainment in every individual. This belief has been the guiding force in a career that spans a half-century of Christian ministry, made me a radio and television personality, speaking on radio daily since 1927, and with over 1200 appearances on local and network television; an international lecturer, author of nearly a score of books, and hundreds of magazine articles. After serving first as magazine editor, then editor-in-chief of the publications of Unity School of Christianity for eleven years, I felt the urge to return to a more personal ministry, and boldly set out to establish such a ministry in Los Angeles; a ministry in which there would be no dues or pledges, but everything sustained by freewill offerings. Starting from scratch in 1938, by March of 1942, three months after Pearl Harbor, I had acquired a church edifice, contracting to pay for it in twenty years. Actually it was paid for in less than two.

"Wealthy backers?"

"No, not unless you would think of God as a Wealthy Backer — and you should, for it is the truth! However, the channels of His supply were not a few wealthy parishioners but many, many people in modest circumstances. It was with their help that the church was paid for. And with God's help the congregation grew to a membership of 8500 in the twenty-seven years of my ministry there; the largest Unity church in the world."

Every Good Desire has a very special significance to me, as the reader will discover. I have quoted the theme statement on which the title is based to thousands of students in my classes and lectures. During the early years of the Los Angeles ministry some of my thoughts on this theme were printed locally for my congregation. Now, for the first time, and in expanded, contemporary form they reach a nationwide readership through my most-admired New York publisher, Harper & Row.

Every Good Desire

1
Every Good Desire

Desire is prophetic of its own fulfillment.

Andrew Jackson Davis

The Turning Point

Good fortune often sneaks up on us at unawares. It may even appear to be misfortune. It may come to you at a time when every door seems closed against you, in ways and through channels that you could not foresee; or it may come in the most ordinary way, so very ordinary that you would not have even considered it. But it comes, and sometimes it even gives an unrecognized hint that it is on the way.

You follow a hunch. You turn a corner.

You read a book, or make a phone call, or meet an old acquaintance or a stranger, and something unforeseeable, unpredictable but logical occurs.

I know, because it has happened to me, not just once but many times through the years.

Time of Challenge

The most striking such turning point came when I was in my upper teens. Illness and misfortunes caused us to move from one of the larger cities in Minnesota to a suburb where rents were lower. I surrendered, at least for the time, my hopes of further schooling, and looked for a job. On the long interurban rides to and from town, I would brood over the situation, ask myself, like Balaam's ass, "What have I done" that this should come upon me?

Plans for the future seemed shattered. I stopped going to church, and broke off the personal associations that actually I needed more than ever, although of

2

course I didn't realize that then.

"I don't know what to do. I don't know where to turn!" I cried to myself, miserably. And it was as if a voice said silently, "Turn within!" And I don't even know how to do that was my responsive thought.

Then one Saturday night I read in the paper that a visiting minister from Southern California was to speak the next afternoon at a vesper service at the very church I had attended. Unaccountably I felt a strong urge to attend the meeting.

That night there was a heavy snowstorm. I waded through snowdrifts up to my knees on my way to the interurban car line. Transportation was slowed by the weather, and the church service had already begun when I slipped into a seat near the back and over a floor register whose heat would help dry my dampened pants legs.

Every Good Desire

The speaker was talking about the compassion and providence of God. That He withholds from us no good thing that mind and heart can envision. *"Every good desire of the heart shall be fulfilled, either in ways that we anticipate, or in other ways that in God's sight are even better."* I drank in his words. I had never heard a minister talk like that.

Suddenly he interrupted his train of thought:

"It is very strange that I should have left my rose-bowered church in Southern California to come to this northern clime at this time of year, but I feel as if I have come here for just one person!"

I suppressed an exclamation. It was as if someone had punched me in the solar plexus. "Why, I am the one!" I exclaimed to myself. It seemed incredible. My conscious mind immediately denied it. Imagination, conceit, wishful thinking! "Don't you imagine that half the people in the congregation are thinking the same

4

thing?'' Nevertheless I could not dismiss the feeling. I waited until the meager congregation had dispersed, then shyly approached the minister.

''I am the one,'' I said.

''Your name wouldn't be Wilson, would it?'' he asked.

''Why yes. But how would you know that?''

''Your minister warned me against you. He said you were unreliable. Where have you been? I've been expecting to see you. I thought any one boy who was important enough for me to be warned against is someone I should know. We're going to be friends. Would you like to do the kind of work I'm doing?''

''It would be wonderful of course. But I couldn't do it.''

''You can if you want to enough!'' was his famous response.

In how many times, how many ways, I was to learn that fortunately I could not know!

Someone has said that faith and fear are pretty much the same. One or the other kept me going; fear that if I ever admitted failure I'd never have the faith to try again.

So when people would ask me to do some "impossible thing," I could only swallow deeply and say I would try; and things turned out right often enough to encourage me. Besides, I *learned* even where I did not succeed as well as I'd have liked; so even those experiences were not total failure.

Sometimes in the face of a baffling situation, I'd think, "I wonder what in the world God's going to do about this!" Often He hasn't done what I might have thought He would — but much better and in surprising ways.

"Richly All Things"

Is there "a divinity that shapes our ends, rough-hew them how we will"? I think there must be. For instance, I think of a man whom I came to know years later. He had become discouraged with the way his life was going. Finally, so he told me, he resorted to the old-fashioned custom of taking the Bible in his hands, praying for guidance, opening it and placing his finger on a text at random. The text proved to be I Timothy, chapter six, beginning with the seventeenth verse. In it Paul was admonishing Timothy to tell the rich not to be proud nor place their trust in their material possessions, because these were unstable, but to put their pride and trust in God, "who giveth us richly all things to enjoy."

This was a far cry from the form of faith in which he had been reared; that piety and poverty were practically inseparable, that the true believer gloried in infirmities, and that joy was almost sinful.

"Who giveth us richly all things to enjoy!"

It had the same kind of impact on him that "every good desire" had on me. He read on to the end of the chapter: do good, share, communicate, form a good foundation on which to build your life.

He had always pictured himself living on a scale that was utterly beyond anything but his imagination, one in which he could provide all things good for his family. Always before he had attempted sternly to reject such thoughts as sinful fantasy. Now the words of Paul put a new light on such imaginings. Instead of thinking of himself in terms of limitation, he began to picture himself and his loved ones as joyous, prosperous, loving, sharing, communicating, serving. He gave more thought to improving their modest home, taking better care of the garden, considering a second car.

Then his plans were shattered. The company for which he worked wanted to move him to a small community in the Middle West. With many misgivings he prepared his family for the move. "Who giveth us richly all things" receded from his mind in the face of this new challenge.

Things turned out better than he could have dreamed. The plant to which he was assigned was in a rural setting. It was surrounded by widespread lawns, a swimming pool, a golf course, tennis courts. The residence assigned him and his family was on a rise of land that spread all this before it. "It is all like a dream come true — only better!" he exclaimed.

His experience reminds me of something a reader had written to me in response to a magazine article of mine she found helpful: *"God opens ways where to human sense there seems to be no way."*

It Could Be You

So I can say with a whole heart, "It could be you!" The Bible tells us that God is no respecter of persons. I take this to mean that He doesn't play favorites; that no matter who you are, or where you are, or what you are, He will help you; that your desire is prophetic of its own fulfillment, if only you want it enough, and find a sense of values and a sense of direction, and follow persistently where they lead.

Yes, every good desire of the heart can be fulfilled. Nothing hoped for is too good to be true; in fact most of what we conceive to be our desire is only a half-truth, which greater understanding will perfect. If there is any secret to attaining such fulfillment, it is this:

Persist: "You can if you want to enough."

Sometimes it is just as well that we don't know at the start of some enterprise just how much effort it entails. If I had known, for instance, how much it would require of me to learn to speak in public I doubt if I would have had the intestinal fortitude to keep trying. The first time I attempted to speak in that little Minnesota church I've mentioned, I had stage fright to such a degree that I had to leave the chancel and lose my breakfast. But "I can't go on being a failure all my life," I declared.

It's an axiom that horseback riders who lose their seat or are thrown must always get up immediately — if indeed that is possible — and ride again. I felt I could do that more readily than return to the pulpit to continue my discourse. But that is what I did.

In whatever we attempt to do that is worthwhile or outstanding, there comes a point when the easiest thing of all is to give up. "Nobody," we may say, "can condemn me for not continuing a project in the face of so many obstacles. Nobody but ourself. Neither talent, nor education, nor training, nor preparation, nor all of them put together can take the place of simple, sheer, plain persistence!

Genius, that power that dazzles mortal
  eyes,
Is oft but perseverance in disguise

wrote Henry Willard Austin.

One man, whose success in his chosen field puzzled his competitors, was the subject of much speculation among them. "How do you account for his success? He has no special gifts. He has no outstanding abilities. He is retiring to a point of shyness. In a field where he is often called upon to address large groups of people, others can talk rings around him. He has no wealthy backers. He often turns opportunities for profit over to others when he might hold on to them to his own advantage. He gives away in a year more than some of us make. Yet he seems to prosper and has the largest work of its kind in the world. It doesn't make sense."

Of course all this did make sense, and one man who had known him through most of his career explained it in just three words: "He works hard."

H. R. Kopmeyer is one who understands that principle. "Do the thing, and you will have the power," he says. Again, "When everything else fails, *try hard work!*" Of course we all know of some persons who work very hard and yet are not very successful. But it is more difficult to find someone who is very successful who has not, at some point along the way, worked very hard. He probably still does, only now the results are more apparent to others than is the effort.

Few people do anything right the first time, or if they do it is by happy accident, like the duffer at golf who makes a hole in one his first time round the course. His initial success may serve as an incentive to pursue the game further, but he soon finds out that there is "hard work" even in a game, though because it's a game, he doesn't call it hard work. Neither, we might add, does the business or professional man who achieves an outstanding success. Hard work is merely a term we use to describe what is a willing, even eager dedication. It may bring him fortune, but he would probably do it regardless.

Successful persons are often the least able to define the reasons for their success. "Ninety-five percent of the people who work for success are failures; what did the other five percent work for?" someone has said.

Fulfillment

Fulfillment may come in either expected or unexpected ways. God will use any channel that is open to Him, as water will take any course that leads it to the sea.

Don't disparage the commonplace, or a "common place." Centuries ago many missed knowing Jesus the Christ because they reasoned, "What, can any good come out of Nazareth?"

It is human nature to be afraid

sometimes in the face of uncertainties, or apparent unpleasant certainties; but the higher potential within us enables us to face our fears and overcome them.

As we attune our thoughts, feelings, and attitudes to accord with the upward, progressive movement of life, all things good become possible, and only the good is enduringly true.

Something or someone has led you to this book.

Turning its pages may be like taking a turn in your life toward the fulfillment of ''every good desire.''

MEDITATION

I have within me the resources to meet the challenges and opportunities that are before me. I go forward to meet them. I face them with confidence. I rejoice in the anticipation of fulfillment and delight in every step that leads to it.

Nothing and no one can keep from me

the good that God has for me. Nothing to which the mind and heart aspire is too good to be true. Most things, as seen through temporal vision, are not quite as good as the ultimate good that God has for me. I cannot hope too much, or expect too much, if I put intelligent, loving, persistent effort back of my aspirations, and work with God for right fulfillment.

2
Your Hidden Channel of Help

*We are adequate and more than
adequate for the circumstances
we are called upon to meet in life*

By In-Direction

Some of the most helpful things we learn
about the fine art of living come about by
in-direction, direction from within.

We labor with some project and don't
seem to get anywhere. We "give up," and
then somehow mysteriously, without
conscious effort, the answer to our need
appears. Our hidden channel of help, the
subconscious mind, is at work!

It was in my effort to help a man who
was in deep trouble, and in the outcome of
the effort which was humanly gratifying,

that I became most impressively aware of a serendipity in the experience: the way of virtually effortless achievement, the unforeseen help of the subconscious.

At that period in my ministry, my counseling office or study was at the end of a long marble hall. Often the click of a person's heels on the marble floor was like the announcement of an approaching visitor. On one such occasion the steps sounded somewhat faltering and uneven. When their producer appeared in my doorway, I could understand why. He was stoned. But he said he wanted help and he believed that I could help him. So I could not settle for a faith less than his.

Early in my ministry I had a series of counseling sessions that greatly influenced my subsequent ministry. One after another I was appealed to by several persons — I think it was six — who believed themselves to be possessed by evil spirits, like the demoniac of Jesus' time. I could not seem to help these afflicted people. I was only twenty at the time, in the very first year of my ministry, and unprepared for such encounters.

So I prayed to God not to let anybody get to me for counseling that I could not help. There were, I reasoned, too many other ministers and counselors from whom they might get more help than I could give. I vowed that if God would do this, I would "know" that if somebody got to me for counseling, it was because I could help him, and I would do my uttermost to do so.

This involves an assumption on my part that God heard and agreed to my appeal. At any rate I have acted upon that assumption through the years.

My faith that that agreement with the Lord — surely the Lord of my own being — was not terminated was challenged by my encounters with this alcoholically addicted man. Time after time he came persistently, but persistently alcoholic, to have me pray with him. I was running out of prayers, or so it seemed. Finally, and more or less desperately, I said, "This time let's have a silent prayer," and in that silence I implored, "Father, take over. I've done all that I know to do!" And with that it was as if the clouds of my troubled human nature parted. The answer appeared so obvious that I wondered why I hadn't thought of it before.

Our previous meetings indicated that despite his addiction my earnest friend was a good worker. He was foreman in an automotive production firm where he had charge over a large number of workmen. I told him about the centurion who came to Jesus and pleaded with him to heal his youthful servant who was in bed and wracked with pain. The centurion said in effect:

"If you will only say, 'Be healed,' my servant will get well I know, because I have authority over my soldiers, and I can say to one, 'Go,' and he goes, and to another, 'Come,' and he comes, and to my slave boy, 'Do this or that,' and he does it. And I know you have authority to tell his sickness to go — and it will go."

"*You* can be like that," I told my inebriated friend. "Like the centurion, you too are a man in authority. You can say to your men, 'Go!' and they will go,

'Do this or that,' and they will do it. If you can do that with the men under your charge, you certainly can do it with even more authority to your own inner forces and faculties. You are too intelligent, too strong a man, too desirous of being your best self — as your repeated sessions with me testify — to let any physical craving have dominion over you.

"I never thought of it like that," he exclaimed. "Will you tell me that again?"

I hoped for that miracle-of-counseling, the Instant Healing. It wasn't. But soon there came the day when the click of his heels as he approached my door was steadier, more regular. He fairly burst into my study. "Doc, it's a miracle," he said. "I only get drunk once a week now!"

The Measure of a Man

You cannot measure a man by where he is at the moment. You must know how far he has come, what direction he is going, how many times he has tried, how much he has overcome.

To get drunk once a week may not sound very impressive as an attainment, but it was a giant step from the virtually constant state of inebriation that preceded it. It proved to that man, "You can succeed, if you know the power that is within you. You can if you want to enough!" He proved to me that he wanted to. He proved to himself that he could. It wasn't too long until he was a free man, free at least from the addiction to drink!

We are tempted to judge others by what they do or fail to do, rather than by what they are and can become. I suppose that distinction is what Jesus was getting at when He said (John 7:24), "Judge not according to the appearance, but judge righteous judgment."

How would you prefer to be judged? By where you are right now? By some incident of past success? Even by all you have been and done since childhood and to the present moment? Is even all this as far as you are capable of going, as much as you can do? Are you not more than any of this, or all of it?

In the long view we are endowed with

infinite possibilities, which inspired the Psalmist (8:4 - 6) to exclaim, "What is man, that thou art mindful of him? and the son of man, that thou visitest him? For thou hast made him a little lower than the angels, and hast crowned him with glory and honour. Thou madest him to have dominion over the works of thy hands; thou hast put all things under his feet."

"Madest Him to Have Dominion"!

Sometimes I think these words are the most important words in the Bible! But of course what are the most important words to any one of us are the ones seen by us to be most closely related to our level of perception, and what we are trying by the grace of God to attain.

Like the Centurion

We are, or are intended to be, like that centurion. Or like Bartimaeus, who had been blind, and who when he received his sight was heckled by those who questioned the healing ("Maybe you only imagined you were blind") or its source ("Maybe it wasn't God but the devil who healed you") and could only cry out, "One thing I know, whereas I was blind, now I see!"

A Marvelous Servant

To the inebriate the remarkable part of our relationship was that he found his own dominion.

To me there was a serendipity in that I discovered by actual experience, rather than by precept only, how marvelously the subconscious mind comes to our aid.

To some persons the subconscious is an unknown quantity.

To others it is the very "Lord of their being."

To still others it is a convenient coverall or catchall into which we may attribute all the difficult-to-explain operations of man's mental and emotional nature.

Fortunately we do not have to wait for an understanding of why it helps as it does, to experience the help that it gives.

In greater or lesser degree we all experience the way the subconscious works.

You try to recall a phone number. It seems to shimmer vaguely in the back of your thoughts. The harder you try to bring it into focus the more elusive it becomes. You still want the number, but your efforts seem futile. You give up trying, your attention is diverted elsewhere, and then up comes the number as if it were a filing card popping up in a filing case. You exclaim, "How could I have forgotten that!" Actually you hadn't; it was submerged beneath the phase of mind we call "conscious," recorded nonetheless in the subconscious.

An equally common but more difficult-to-explain experience is that in which we find ourselves suddenly thinking of someone out of context with current trends of thought. In a moment the phone rings. The person we had suddenly thought of is on the line. Or we feel the urge to phone or write to some acquaintance we have not thought about for a long time, and get the response, "How did you know that I was meeting a special experience right at that time, and that word from you would be reassuring?"

Is it stretching credulity too far to think that as we reach toward the center of being our subconscious on occasion makes contact with that of other kindred souls? As concerted human attention turns from outer space to inner space, we shall no doubt find more about *why* such things occur. *That* they occur is already established.

The reach of such experience is extensive.

Adela Rogers St. Johns tells in one of her books how her friend, Paul Gallico, was trying to complete a story that would not jell. "I could get it started," he said, "but I couldn't finish it. . . . I had just about given this story up — in fact, had forgotten it — when suddenly one night during a symphony concert I was attending in Carnegie Hall the solution popped out of nowhere and the story simply rolled forth."

My friend, Charles "Chuck" Reisner, told me the story of how, having been lured away from a successful career as a motion picture director in Hollywood by offers that kept him in Europe for two years, he returned to find every door seemingly closed to him. "Out to lunch, in conference, on vacation, not in production, don't call us, we'll call you," were the rebuffs that turned him away. The climax was reached for him emotionally when his young man son, who since has made a prominent place for himself in the industry, remarked, "Dad, the parade has passed you by."

After a sleepless night at his apartment in Hollywood, he decided his son was right and got in his car and started down the Coast Highway toward his cottage in Laguna Beach. Idly he turned on his car radio and heard a voice saying, "Man was born not to defeat but to victory. You can succeed. Try again.'' He parked the car by the roadside and listened till the program changed, then made a U-turn and started back to Hollywood. On impulse, he went to the gates of the great studio where he had once been a top director. Every door opened before him. He was ushered into the office of The Big Man. ''Chuck, you're just the man we've been looking for. We're having trouble with a script. Will you take a look at it, and see what you can do with it?''

Reisner took the script with him back to his Franklin Avenue apartment, worked it over, and was asked to return to the studio to direct a picture with some popular comedians who were rated high at the box office but were notably difficult to work with. ''Strange to say, production went forward without a hitch,'' he told me. It was the first of a series of successful assignments.

We used to say, years ago, ''Man's extremity is God's opportunity.'' Now we say it is the evocation of the subconscious.

Like a Computer

Evoking the help of the subconscious mind is very much like the way a computer works. You put into it all the pertinent material, even apparently irrelevant items; then you push a button or pull a lever, dismiss the matter from your mind, and pretty soon the computer comes up with the needed solution or way to proceed.

There is a time for concentrated attention to our problems. But there is also — and probably in equal measure — a time for relaxation, for going to a symphony or a ball game, or for a hike in the woods, or idle sitting on a rock and looking out over the valley or hills or city or sea; a time, as Walt Whitman said, to loaf and invite the soul. The subconscious frees the conscious mind to deal with current demands and creative thought. But a scent, the lilt of a melody, the sound of a locomotive whistle or a foghorn often will call back to remembrance some long forgotten incident. Not only that, but it will often complete a train of unfinished thought, and can do it more effectively than the conscious mind.

Thoreau evidently understood this. He writes in his Journal, "The really efficient laborer will be found not to crowd his day with work, but will saunter to his task surrounded by a wide halo of ease and leisure."

Lowell Fillmore, in a poem called "The Answer," writes in part, "When for a purpose I had prayed and prayed and prayed. . . . And all my fervor and persistence brought no hope, I paused to give my weary brain a rest. . . . And, lo, my prayer was answered in that hour."

The trouble is we work too hard with our conscious mind. We do not do as well or accomplish as much, as if we were using our whole mental equipment, and were *letting* the subconscious mind relieve us of much of the conscious stress and strain of daily decisions, bringing to us the stored up knowledge and experience of the past, and leaving us more time for relaxation and creativity.

Indeed it appears to be able to bring more than these. It brings up even things that have never been consciously known before, and often oñ subjeects that are new in human experience, and only indirectly related to the goals of the persons to whom they come.

Many musicians will tell you that their most successful compositions come unsought, while they are seated at a desk or instrument, thinking idly or in reverie. Scientists make discoveries in a similar way, often to their own great surprise. Not infrequently such new ideas come to them in dreams.

It was soon after the turn of the century that Professor William James, renowned as one of the great thinkers of America, declared the discovery of the subconscious mind to be the greatest discovery in a hundred years. It has been variously derided and acclaimed; its full significance is not yet charted, but seems so vast as to approach the miraculous. We shall have to leave the intricacies of such explorations to others.

Sufficient for most of us is to become

aware of its helpfulness and to learn how to avail ourselves of its help.

Among my notes, I find three such methods, ascribed to Robert R. Updegraff: "Give your problems to your subconscious mind in the form of definite assignments.

"One method is to write down on a sheet of paper whatever problems that are facing you, jotting down all the important factors. If there are pros and cons to be dealt with, put them in parallel columns. Read them over without trying to come to any conclusion, and *tear up the paper and forget all about it.*

"Talk over the entire situation or problem with close associates or members of the family. *Get right down to cases but don't come to any conclusions.* End the discussion abruptly, and set the whole matter aside to 'simmer.'

"A third method is to work consciously on the problem until you are plumb fagged out mentally. At that point *put it entirely out of your mind.* Go fishing, hunting, motoring, or, if it is night, go peacefully to bed."

MEDITATION

I am adequate and more than adequate for the daily adventures in living that come to me. Guided by the innate Knower within me I know what to accept and what to reject. I am positive against all that is beneath or unworthy of me, receptive to all that is above. I am receptive, responsive, and obedient to guidance. Nothing and no one can keep from me the good that God has for me. I rejoice in the good that comes to others as though to me. I adopt a listening attitude, tuning in to a recognition of the order, harmony, and progressive purpose of the universal life of which my life is a part. I am grateful for all channels of help and inspiration from the world about me; most of all for "that gleam of light that flashes across the firmament from within" me.

3
Blue Monkeys

You may never have heard of them, but by this name or some other, or none, everyone has to deal with them—and can.

How They Got Their Name

It is a law older than man that like attracts like, so I suppose it was almost inevitable that a wily guru and an impressionable student who aspired to become a spiritual teacher should come together.

What did they have in common that should attract them to each other?

They were both, in different ways, greedy.

The guru was in what people sometimes call "straitened circumstances," in a word, penniless, but determined not to remain so if his guile could get him out of it.

The student was convinced that there must be some shortcut to the goal of eminence he desired to reach. He did not so much want to become spiritually eminent as to become spiritually affluent. He was eager and assiduous. He faithfully performed all manner of physical and mental exercises that the guru had learned or could invent, over a longer period of time than he had anticipated, until both his credulity and his financial resources were approaching exhaustion.

Finally the wily guru realized that the humbug could not be sustained much longer.

"You have now acquired all the wisdom that I can give you," he declared. "Faithfully follow the instructions I have offered, and you will reap fantastic rewards. But one thing I must caution you against. Never, ever, allow yourself to think of blue monkeys, or all the lore I've taught you will be in vain. You will be little wiser than when you came to me!"

And the student did no mighty works, because of course he could think of nothing but blue monkeys whenever he tried to work the guru's spells.

Creative Imagination

You are the victim of blue monkeys whenever you allow yourself to think, regarding some good desire, "It is too good to be true," or "I don't know the right people," or any one of the limiting mental and emotional attitudes which decree failure before you have even tried. Imagination is a two-edged sword. Directed constructively it can lead to many wonderful things. Allowed to take a fearful, defeatist direction it can be a deterrent to all good attainment. Gird yourself, therefore, with incessant affirmatives. Affirm, *"My desire is prophetic of its own fulfillment. Every good desire shall be fulfilled, either in ways that I now see, or in other ways that are even better. Nothing can keep my good from me. I can, I will, I do!"*

Defeating Blue Monkeys

Is there a blue monkey in your life?

"My mother has one," a friend of mine tells me. "It was the fear of an incurable illness. When I was a small boy my mother took me with her to my grandmother's house. Mother nursed her through two years of illness. In those days cancer was such a dreaded affliction that no one ever called the illness by its name. It was not until years later that I was allowed to know. But from time to time through the years, whenever my mother had an ache or pain, I would observe the frightened look that came over her face, and I came to realize what she was thinking: 'Am I going to die of cancer too?' When finally, well in her eighties, she did pass away, she merely complained of a tight feeling around her heart and asked for an aspirin, and before it could be gotten and given to her she expired. I've often thought how sad it seems that mother suffered so much, so many times, of something that never happened except in her anxious imaginings!''

Every now and then we read of someone living alone in relative squalor, who following his demise is found to have a sizable fortune in a safety deposit vault in a bank, or even worse, hidden away in tin cans or among the pitiful belongings of his humble abode.

One acquaintance who has a bald pate is troubled by the thought that others depreciate him because of this; another has a very sensitive skin which gives him trouble whenever he becomes emotionally upset; another, who normally speaks slowly and deliberately in ordinary circumstances, will become flushed of face and addicted to stuttering and stammering when called upon to meet and converse with strangers.

To one such person, who confided his distressed feelings to a good friend, came the heartening response, ''I'm not a psychologist or physician, but I can help you with that; just remember that nobody notices much but you!''

There is something about monkeys, blue or otherwise (and thoughts that are of the same obsessive character) that can be invaluable to know. It is illustrated by the story of a man exploring a tropical jungle. He became weary from groping his way through the dense growth of shrubs and vines, and coming upon a pleasant open grass plot, lay down to rest. He fell asleep and was awakened by an incessant chattering that seemed to come from the branches of nearby trees.

The trees were filled with monkeys.

The venturesome ones began to clamber down from the treetops and surround him. Alarmed, he rose and tried to move away from them. They followed him, some from the ground around him, some swinging from the branches of the trees. The faster he went, the more aggressively they pursued. He broke into a run, stumbled, and fell. They stopped, regarding him. On impulse he rose and inadvertently moved toward them, and they turned and fled, disappearing from sight, silently.

Blue monkeys or their relatives always

tend to enter into our meditations. It is important to know how to deal with them because everyone needs to have some time each day when he "comes to himself." The busier our life pattern, the greater the need, whether we call that quiet time prayer, meditation, reverie, the silence, or just catching up with our thinking. Perhaps you begin by deliberately releasing your conscious thought from the pressures of the day. Perhaps you turn to a line or two of verse, a Bible passage, an affirmation, or maybe just a word that expresses a theme, such as love, faith, freedom. What actually happens?

Blue monkeys!

The thought of a person needing help, or the urgency of a financial need, or the desire to resolve a misunderstanding comes persistently, naggingly, when you are trying, perhaps to be "very spiritual," to think only of the beautiful, the good, the true. Unlike the story of the guru and the student, these blue monkeys are your very own; they are part of your own life pattern. They well up from the subconscious to which you have tried to confine them. Then as soon as the intensity of your conscious thought abates, they take the opportunity to bob up, and say in effect, "What about me?" If you try to evade or avoid them, if you take refuge in sleep, they will only persist, even to the point of appearing in your dreams.

Face them and the pressure eases. Invite them into your reverie. Say or think, with feeling for the person needing help, *"The Creative Principle within you is mightier than anything that affronts or affrights you from without or within. God is your help in every need, and in the need of this moment. My loving thought joins with yours to bring you peace of body, soul, and spirit."*

If it is a financial need, dwell on a thought such as this: *"All barriers of financial limitation are now dissolved; God is my instant, constant, and abundant supply of all good. I give as I would receive, richly, promptly, abundantly. God opens ways of fulfillment and recompense where there may even seem to be none. I invite ideas of usefulness and service. I do a wonderful work in a wonderful way, I give wonderful service for wonderful pay. Plenty is mine, for I am a child of the Most High, who is fullness and completeness."*

Does the thought of a misunderstanding claim recognition? Declare, *"All the barriers of misunderstanding are now dissolved. Goodwill and a friendly spirit can bridge any communication gap. The best in me greets the best in you. I trust in that nature to find expression. Let forgiveness, clear thought, good feeling be manifest in all concerned; and let it begin with me."*

Often people say that when they try to meditate or pray on a lofty plane, they either become sleepy or their thought wanders. The secret of this is, frankly, lack of interest on the one hand, or a lapse into the negation of self-indulgence with problem-thinking. When you welcome your blue monkeys into this inner circle of reverie, you are reaching the place in consciousness "where the action is."

All the good thoughts, feelings, concepts with which your reverie or meditation begins are like turning on light in your personal world. Light can enter darkness and dissolve it. Darkness cannot enter light. So turn the light on anything that appears dark in the limbos of your inner nature. When you yourself are in darkness, as when there is a power failure, or the flashlight doesn't work, what do you want most? Light. Your blue monkeys come not to frighten, harass, or disturb the calm peace of your soul. They are drawn to the light your thoughts and feelings have engendered. Do not reject them, nor fear them. Deal with them lightly.

The method is practical and rewarding. It works.

MEDITATION

I am not dismayed or overcome by adverse appearances. I am one with the all-embracing, all-infolding good. I radiate that good in thought and feeling, word and action. I know that for every positive action initiated by me, there is an equal and positive reaction. I envision myself as being in the right place at the right time, doing the right thing in the right way. I concentrate my thoughts, feelings, energies upon purposeful, constructive activity. I invite good outcomes in response to the good investment of my inner resources. I do not dictate the channels through which my good shall come to me. I recognize that it comes in both expected and unexpected ways, without haste, without delays, in perfect ways. The good I seek is seeking me. I welcome it and share it.

4
Effortless Concentration

"What do I concentrate on? Oh, just everything!"

Mind Thinks

The nature of the mind is to think.

To keep the mind from thinking is a virtual impossibility. Mystics, who try to "still" the mind so that a Greater Mind may take over, claim to hold thought in suspension for even a few seconds is a colossal effort; that the record is five seconds — although how they could know this for sure is not clear. There is a constant stream of thought that flows through your consciousness. Haphazard thinking is letting the mind float on this stream without direction or purpose. Many persons do not know that this stream can be modified, controlled, directed, applied for constructive purposes. And of course many who know or suspect that this is so, lack the will or singleness of purpose, the discipline, to apply the truth they know.

Directed thinking is the use of your power to change the nature and direction of the stream. It is choosing your thoughts rather than simply reacting to whatever comes along, or "waiting for something to turn up." Untidy minds are without order. They are like a warehouse where the goods are stored without a plan or purpose. Concentration is a way of choosing the goods and establishing order.

To concentrate means to bring, come to, or direct toward a common center.

Concentration and strain are not the same thing. In fact, strain defeats the purpose. You can guide and direct thought; you can invite it. You cannot compel it. To relax is to invite. Thought does not respond to force. Relaxation is a prerequisite to concentration. When you see someone with his face all distorted by effort of thought, and he tells you he is concentrating, applaud his effort, but deplore his method.

When you first attempt to concentrate — to choose and direct your thoughts — you may find it difficult to keep your mind on what you are doing. Your thoughts, like undisciplined children, tend to wander off in all directions. Calmly but resolutely bring them back to whatever you choose to be the center of your concern of the moment. If you have many activities, all may have a claim upon your attention. But you make the decision. You choose what shall take precedence. Affirm, *"This one thing I do. I am the lord of my mentality and the ruler of my thought people. . . . I can say to a hundred, 'Go,' and they will go; to another hundred, 'Come,' and they will come,"* as the centurion did.

Idle thoughts can be summarily dismissed, but the serious ones are there for a purpose. If they are of a negative or destructive character, they should not be rejected nor can they be wisely ignored. They are like wanderers straying in darkness. When you turn purposeful attention to your conscious thoughts, it is like turning on light in darkness. Whatever is in darkness seeks the light. (How wonderful the provision of nature that light can enter darkness, but darkness cannot enter light.)

Aids to Concentration

Most things do not take very long to do or are not very hard to do when the way is prepared for them. "The difficult can be done instantly, the impossible takes a little longer," someone has said. Here are some things that prepare the way, that make effortless concentration a reality instead of a vagary.

1. Consent to the concept that whatever commands your attention is worthy of it. By doing this you can clear the way for effortless concentration. It is like clearing the riverbed of that stream of thought that you are choosing and

directing. You make it the open channel through which the inspiration and action of the Knower can manifest. Invite and invoke the Knower to shed light upon whatever need or problem is involved. The answer may come immediately; it may be deferred; do not let it be ignored. Affirm, "My mind is one with the All-knowing Mind, the Knower, who brings all things needful to my remembrance and understanding." It is like a light that makes clearer things that were obscure. I do not wander off into the darkness, I bring things to light.

2. Affirm your oneness with the Knower as the All-infolding Good. You thereby raise your consciousness to a higher level of awareness and response. Your horizon of thought and feeling widens. You see things more clearly and in a broader view. You envision yourself as one with, a part of, the universal good. Look for that good in whatever you contemplate.

3. Remember that there is no effort or strain in contemplating anything that is beautiful, complete, or perfect; rather, to do so blesses your eyes, your mind,

perhaps your heart.

Lillian Gish, a famous motion picture actress of the early Hollywood days, preserved a kind of aura of inward serenity and peace in the midst of all the orderly chaos incident to setting up a scene to be screened, by contemplating a single rose which she held in her hand.

A minister, called on short notice to offer a midnight New Year's Eve prayer on a set where band members, singers, and announcers were setting up props and prompter's cards all around him, was approached by one of the performers. "You're the only one here who seems to be calm and at peace on this whole huge set!" he exclaimed. The minister responded, "I'm tuning in for what I'll be doing on camera a few minutes from now. Why don't you join me?"

"I cannot help the ladies of the woman's club today; I'm driving out to the seashore to commune with the wind and sea, and get my sense of values readjusted!" a certain ebullient member announced to the club president. She didn't know that it was a help to the club members as well as to herself. She was, like Jurgen's wife, "a well-meaning woman with no great gift for silence" or for tact. She did not realize that her well-meant bluntness was a disturbing element to others. She found it easier to commune with nature than with people; but the one purpose, if accomplished, could truly lead to the other.

Some of our wonderful young people of today who reject the Establishment (though seldom its benefits) turn to nature for surcease from complexities. Though they may find only a temporary release in this way, they may, as many persons of all times have done, find courage, faith, and patience to rejoin and help transform the Establishment, to their own betterment as well.

4. Contemplate a simple picture or a scene until you feel that it is clear in your mind. Then close your eyes and recall every detail of what you have been viewing objectively. If you can recall it with no details missing, you have done extremely well. If not, keep on trying until you succeed. Next time try to

recapture the details of a more complicated subject. When you are visiting a strange office or home, practice the same exercise. When you are meeting an individual or a group of people give your full attention to each one as you are introduced. If you are distracted and do not get a name clearly, ask that it be repeated. Your interest will appear to be complimentary. If you can make an imaginary mental association between some item of the person's appearance and his name, it will help. Even though you may have neither the interest nor occasion to see the person again, you will have gained a point in your power of concentration.

The Paramount Factor

5. Of course interest is the secret. There is little effort involved when you are deeply interested in anything, a person, a place, an object, a name, something that you are reading. Most of us have had the experience of becoming absorbed in

something we are reading; a person enters the room, or speaks, and, as we say, "I jumped out of my skin!" Perhaps this is to say that you "jumped back into your skin," in the sense that you were called back out of a mental-emotional environment into your immediate physical environment. This is somehow related to being summoned back to this objective world when, as you are drifting off to sleep, a sound or movement recalls you to the waking state and you have the sensation of falling, as from a height, onto the bed.

You may have to make a special effort when a reason for interest is not apparent.

6. Various forms of affirmative suggestion are a well-attested aid to concentration. *Think adverbially:* Instead of dwelling on Love, for example, think *lovingly* of persons, things, events that are vital to your sense of well-being; Peace, Joy, Harmony the same, peacefully, joyously, harmoniously. *Personalize an abstract thought:* Instead of merely affirming, "God is my

help in every need," make it pragmatic by adding "and in the need of this moment." *Lasso stray thoughts:* If your thoughts still tend to wander, do not wander with them. Bring them into the light of the intended purpose. (This is the blue monkey aspect of concentration again!) *Alive, awake, alert!* Do you become sleepy when you try to concentrate? This might be the result of having become accustomed to working under tension to such a degree that when you begin to relax, the body grasps the opportunity to recuperate from the tension. In that case take a few moments simply to relax physically as well as mentally and emotionally before you attempt to concentrate. The affirmative aids here given are a kind of exercise in relaxation. But if you get sleepy it may be an indication of trying to force an interest in what you are attempting, where no real interest exists.

After all, why should you be interested in effortless concentration, when it seems to require a lot of effort? The effort will become less and less, the ease of concentration greater and greater, once you realize the true importance of developing your concentrative ability. Don't be like the sweet young thing who attended a lecture on Methods of Concentration. Thanking the speaker at the door at the conclusion, she ventured the comment that of course concentration was very easy for her.

"That's interesting. What do you concentrate on?" he asked.

"Oh, just everything!" she responded ecstatically.

Let us hope that the young lady was simply being facetious in her statement. For certainly the person who concentrates on just everything is "ex-centrating" rather than concentrating; scattering his energies rather than directing them. Results are likely to be minimal and disappointing. The way to attainment does not lie in that direction, for it is not a direction.

Concentration —
the Secret of Success

You will succeed greatly in many ways as you develop the power of concentration. Concentration is a frequently misunderstood word. Again, it does not mean strain. It does not mean to fasten your mind on an objective and to try to keep it there. Instead, it is a high degree of voluntary attention to a clearly defined purpose. Don't waste your energies by concentrating on your failures, past or present, or on the "powers and principalities" that loom so large on the horizon. Some of the greatest fortunes have been made during troubling times. Some have been based on the filling of a human need so long endured that almost everyone had taken it for granted. Almost! Until someone wondered "What would happen if —" and gave the matter such concentrated, contemplative attention that he became the open channel for a breakthrough, an innovative idea and its expression.

Glenn Clark tells in his little book, *The*

Man Who Talks with Flowers, the story of his visit with the famous black man, George Washington Carver, who achieved an education against seemingly insuperable odds, and helped many other young black men to get an education. Carver became concerned about the dependency of the southern states on cotton, their one and only, but variable, crop. He discovered a hundred and fifty different products derived from peanuts, almost as many for yams, both of which grew readily in the poor soil of the area.

Doctor Clark asked him how he had ever attained such wisdom. Doctor Carver asserted that the peanut talked to him and told him what to do.

"How is that possible? How can you communicate with the peanut?" was the challenging question.

Doctor Carver's answer was a remarkably simple description of the concentrative process. "First you have to be very humble, next you have to love the object of your quest, and finally you have to be expectant." He claimed that love will open the way to knowledge; that what you humbly, deeply, expectantly love will reveal its secrets, even a peanut, a yam, a weed — or perhaps a person!

Not Magic, but Essential

All great people are great concentrators. Quite probably no matter how much we concentrate, how diligently and purposefully we apply our abilities and resources we will not all attain equal results, for it must be said that we are not all created equal, despite the familiar statement, except in the sight of God. We don't all bring with us at birth the same talents or abilities. Some are born into a race that is predominant in its part of the world; others to a less favored race; some are born into normal, beautifully endowed bodies; others to bodies afflicted; some into a family of love and affluence, others into a broken and poverty-stricken environment.

But learning the technique of contemplative concentration will enable any of us to far exceed what might have reasonably been his lot without that technique.

The methods vary with each individual. Jesus went up to a mountain; Solomon into his sanctuary. Abraham Lincoln did his best concentrating while walking alone in the woods. Woodrow Wilson, when he had a big problem to solve, did his best job of concentrating while reading a detective story. Mark Twain did his best writing sitting up in bed and smoking a big black cigar. Edgar Allen Poe did his best work sitting at his desk and stroking a big black cat. Handel seemed to concentrate best — of all places — in a graveyard. John Emerson had his "little white shrine."

It Could Be You

Fulton thought steamboats, Ford thought automobiles, Rockefeller thought oil, Einstein thought relativity, Lincoln thought union, Darwin thought evolution. Curie thought radium, De Forest thought television, Fermi thought atomic chain reaction, Wiener thought cybernetics, and Nader (who would be surprised to see his name in such company) thought the consumer.

Apparently the Knower will use any channel of mind that is open to Him, as water will use any channel that leads it to its parent sea. A great thought conceivably might come to anyone humble, loving, and expectant enough to be receptive and responsive to it. And it is great ideas in the minds of men that make for the greatness of the nation in which they live and serve.

MEDITATION

In quietness and in confidence I find my strength. I refuse to waste my energies in senseless worry, criticism, or faultfinding. I center my thoughts and feelings upon right outcomes. I dwell upon things that are enduringly true, and let the pattern of their emergence form in my inner world. Without strain or effort, as if beholding a glorious sunset or the tranquil passage of clouds across the sky, I contemplate with tranquillity the orderly sequence by which good follows good, miracle follows miracle, and wonders never cease in my life and my world. From the center of life and light within me, I radiate love and blessing to everyone everywhere.

5
What to Ask For — And How to Get It

There are countless people in the world who do not know what they want from life, how to ask for it, or what to do with it after they get it.

The Easiest Thing?

It would appear that the easiest thing in the world is to know what we want in life. Yet ask anyone what he wants and you will get some peculiar answers.

"I don't know what I want, but I sure can tell you what I don't want!" is one of them. It is a spontaneous answer, no doubt, and one could wish it to be exceptional, but sadly it is a common one, and sadly too it is unproductive, for you can't build on negatives. It is too much like going idly into a shop, and meeting the query, "What can I do for you?" with the answer, "Oh, I don't know. I just want to spend some money!"

Knowing some of the things you don't want can be a step toward finding what you do want, and of how to get it. The path is likely to be found somewhere between those who have no idea and those who have too many or too fixed ideas.

The affirmative answers to the query, "What do you want from life?" are often as superficial as the negative ones.

"I want to be happy," is one of the most common. So you persist by asking, "What do you think will make you happy?" and you get such responses as

— a million dollars,
— a Rolls-Royce,
— marrying into wealth and position,
— freedom from somebody, something,
—health and well being.

Reaching Beyond Things

Why does a man want a million dollars? Would he know how to use the million dollars effectively? Coming into possession of an unaccustomed amount of money may require as much thought and planning in how to make use of it, as were expended in acquiring it. Do you need a Rolls-Royce (which will last you a lifetime) as a kind of status symbol, by which you are assuring yourself (more than others, really) that you are an affluent, capable, successful person, worthy of others' respect and friendship? Or would you actually be more comfortable in a lower-priced car, which is well within your means, and which you could trade in for a new model every couple of years, enjoying the change of color and style as well as the feeling of newness?

And which come first in your life, linking your life with someone you truly love, or trying to love someone whose environment offers promise?

Is not the same principle involved with

situations as with persons? And have not we all at some time thought, "Oh, if I could only flee from this problem"? And perhaps taken steps to do so, only to find a similar situation in the new environment!

And concerning health and well-being: do we seek only freedom from discomfort or pain? Are we like the man who was in hades, and did not plead for freedom from whatever had caused him to be there, but only for water to soothe his parched lips?

"Take what you want from me, and pay for it," Life invites. For we can have whatever we want from Life, if we will pay the price. (Though we do not always see the price tag, or want to.)

You want freedom from someone? A spouse, a friend, a business associate or partner? How shall you achieve this? Have you disentangled yourself from emotional involvements to the point where you can dispassionately consider whether you have learned all you can, contributed all that you can to the association, so that without rancor or guilt or self-justification, you can feel free in thought and emotion? Remember the ancient story of the man who wrestled with an angel and said, ''I will not let thee go except thou bless me!'' Do not we all wrestle with angels — or devils, for the matter of that — and are we ever really free until we discover something we have learned, some service or helpfulness we have rendered, so that we can honestly say, ''It is finished''?

A First Step

So here is a practical first step to take. Make out a list of what you want from life and what you can do to attain it. Read the list over every day for a month. Make changes freely as you feel like it. But don't stop at that. Start out on an interesting adventure of exploring other people's minds and worlds. You might begin at the public library. Examine books and magazines that deal with the subjects in which you are interested. Visit people and organizations devoted to them.

Most everybody feels that he could become a successful writer, if only he had the time for it. There is a story worth telling in almost everybody's life: but getting it down acceptably on paper is another matter. Once in a while, someone without any previous experience in writing will produce a best seller. Once in a very great while! For the same person to do so a second time is even more remarkable. To write successfully and consistently requires something that is involved in any attainment, *preparation,* which we'll have something more to say about later. What is done well appears to be done easily, so much so that trapeze artists and high-wire performers, for instance, will appear almost to fall by way of reminding the viewer of the proficiency required.

Have you made your list? Have you read and reread it, studied it, investigated some of the procedures that are not apparent to the uninformed?

Are you more content with present ways of life? If not, know with confidence that you can attain new goals, for *desire is prophetic of fulfillment.*

The Right Button

"No matter who you are, if you push the right button the light will come on," a business acquaintaince of mine asserts. It is a very ancient concept clothed in modern dress. The Big Fisherman said it in the language of his day some two thousand years ago: "God is no respecter of persons" (Acts 10:34).

It doesn't matter who you are,
It doesn't matter where you are,
It doesn't matter how good or bad
   you have been,
The light will come on.
You will get immediate results.

What you may do with the results of your action is as variable as you are variable from other persons, as predictable as human nature is predictable.

The results may seem magical, because sometimes they are so far beyond expectation, appear in such unexpected ways, and are so immediate. They are not *always* beyond expectation nor immediate; but they are as *sure* as the return of a boomerang or the recoil of a gun or the turning of the tide.

Action and reaction, sowing and reaping, cause and effect, are the manifestation of universal law.

Universal Law

You are invoking the action of a universal law.

Turning on light is an apt symbol for the understanding all of us are seeking in life. Jesus made use of this symbol in many of His sayings: "I am the light of the world." "Ye are the light of the world . . . Let your light so shine." Paul admonished the Ephesians, "Ye were sometimes darkness, but now are ye light in the Lord: walk as children of light."

Even in the light we do not all see with

the same clarity, or even see the same things. The way we see is not only a matter of eyesight but of vision and viewpoint, of what we bring to the light as well as what the light brings to us.

Plato tells the story of a man who was chained on a narrow ledge in an underground cavern, in such a manner that all he saw of others was their shadows cast upon a wall. Finally he broke his chains and groped his way up a winding stair to the brighter light of the upper world. People called him an idiot because he stumbled and groped his way like a blind man; but Plato called him the divine idiot, because his blindness was not the blindness of deepening darkness but of growing sight.

Gaining something we have wanted does not absolve us from responsibility. It does not transform us in the twinkling of an eye from the person we have been into an angelic being (as for instance some people expect death to do); but it may and should make it clear that things do not happen by chance; that this is so much an orderly universe that where we see what seems to be an exception to the rule, we rightfully question the appearance.

From the tiniest electron to worlds whirling through the vast reaches of space there is predictable law and order. Everything brings forth after its kind. As you sow, so shall you reap. Sow the wind and you will reap the whirlwind. What you send out tends to come back to you, increased and multiplied. Sowing and reaping, action and reaction, cause and effect.

In a word, the most efficient way to get what we want from life is to prepare for it. Like the wily little tax gatherer, Zacchaeus, who was curious to know what manner of man Jesus was. So he took the trouble to find out what way Jesus would approach the area, and being short of stature, which may mean short of understanding as well, he climbed up into a fig-mulberry tree whose branches overspread the road on which the Master should approach.

"Come down from there, Zacchaeus," the Master said in effect, "I'm coming home to sup with you!" And the little man almost fell out of the tree in astonishment, and thereby entered upon an experience that changed his whole life.

He "put himself in the way" of finding what he sought, and in doing so found more and better than he sought, which is as true today as in that olden time.

If You Want to Enough

"No matter who tells you otherwise, you cannot get something for nothing." But there is almost no limit to your possible attainments if you want them enough.

How much is enough?

It is better not to know completely in advance. Samuel Johnson said that enthusiasm never sees beyond the down payment; and perhaps that is a very good thing; because if we saw all that was required it might be overwhelming. The saving grace is that all that is required is not all required *at once*. You only have to meet today's challenges today. "Sufficient unto the day is the evil thereof,'' but strength and courage and resources are sufficient too.

Preparation

What, then, shall we ask for, and how can we get it?

The price we pay is preparation, either voluntary or involuntary, coupled with persistence.

Zacchaeus *put himself in the way of finding* what he sought. The Man whom he sought put it very simply, ''As you give, so shall you receive.'' Abraham Lincoln, reading by the light of an open fire or a candle's flame, put it simply: ''I will work and prepare and some day my opportunity will come.'' What preparation and what opportunity! The general rule seems to be that we get pretty much what we are prepared to receive; and if an opportunity comes for which we are not prepared, we are called to do some intensive filling in.

So we see Demosthenes standing on the seashore with pebbles in his mouth, practicing clear speech, and becoming a renowned orator;

Ford, a failure in his fifties, tinkering with his dream of a gasoline engine that was destined to usher in the age of the automobile;

Edison dreaming a thousand dreams of things beyond the vision of other men, and making those dreams come true;

Walt Disney, whose inventive imagination was fascinated by fairy stories and folklore, perfecting methods of picturing and animating them on film; many times on the verge of bankruptcy and failure, but coming through to one of the most amazing success stories of the century;

Others, working as a team, evoking the power that put men on the moon!

You could never be like any of these, you say? You do not have the innate talent, the required resources? Who says so besides yourself, and by what authority? Even the greatest were not the greatest in everything. Einstein, it is said, was very poor at arithmetic, but that did not stop him from developing the theory of relativity.

> Lives of great men all remind us
> We can make our lives sublime,
> And, departing, leave behind us
> Footprints on the sands of time.

So declared the poet Longfellow — and none of these other greats could put thoughts and words together as he did.

Wise men of the past have known these things and taught them, and like wise men of today were sometimes better at pointing the way than going it.

Shakespeare has Portia saying, "If to do were as easy as to know what were good to do, chapels had been churches, and poor men's cottages princes' palaces," and Paul, who was pretty good at laying down the law for others, confesses in his letter to the Romans, "the good that I would I do not: but the evil which I would not, that I do" (7:19).

We suffer most often not from ignorance but from failure to put into practice the constructive, positive, productive things that we do know.

Working With Universal Law

If you think that it is the will of a Supreme Being, the Creative Principle, for you to be unhappy, a failure, sick, inhibited, prone to evil, then so for a time at least it must be so *for you! Until you change your mind.* If you still persist in rejecting the concept of an Oversoul, a Creative Principle of being that has reason, purpose, fulfillment as goals of human attainment, then it is all-important that you should do something about it.

Look about you. You will not have to look far to see the evidence of that Creative Principle at work. Most people in the old Mosaic-Christian ethos still call that Principle "God." With all our modern self-consciousness in such matters as that, the created still must have had a Creator. It is difficult to find a better word than God, spelled with a capital G, for men have had many gods in the past and it has taken too long a time to arrive at the concept of One Presence and One Power to reject it until we can find something better.

That Presence and Power, let us accept, is everywhere present; it keeps the worlds spinning in space, revolving in their orbits; and the pattern is repeated in the smallest worlds our instruments of precision can discern.

It is within man. Not just one Man. All men.

Wherever you are, you can reach God.

Wherever you are, God can reach you.

He is the light of all worlds, and of your world. Zoroaster knew and taught this, Siddhartha Gautama knew and taught it. Jesus declared, "Let your light shine," and Paul admonished, "Walk as children of light."

How long will it take?

The very moment when you accept the concept of universal law and its action in your life, you will begin to get results. For you can become an open channel through which the constructive forces of life are now working.

Wherever you are, you can tune in on

the Creative Principle.

Wherever you are, the Creative Principle can use you as a channel.

Nothing and no one can keep from you what you are prepared to give and to receive.

Affirm, "God opens ways where there seem to be none. I prepare for the good I seek to become manifest in form as I now envision it, or in ways that in God's sight are even better."

MEDITATION

My life activities are an affirmation of the things and events I desire to have appear in my life and my world.

I want health and vitality so I am obedient to the laws of well-being as far as I know and understand them.

I want prosperity, so I give as I would receive, richly, freely, joyously, promptly; and I receive the good that comes to me with praise and thanksgiving.

I want others to understand me, and credit me with good motives in my activities; I try to be understanding of others, their viewpoints, interests, motives.

I want to love and be loved, so I seek to be loving as I would be loved, unselfishly, receptively but not possessively, in the name and nature of the spark of divinity within the beloved.

6
Getting Immediate Results

The difficult can be done immediately,
the impossible takes a little longer.

Instantly!

A popular black comedian is heralded in
the news as an overnight success,
automobiles come off the production line
every few minutes (or is it every few
seconds!), a passenger plane flies faster
than the speed of sound, space capsules
journey to distant planets at 25,000 miles
per hour, electronic ovens produce a cake
in seconds and a roast in three minutes.
We have pre-cooked meals, "heat and
serve," instant tea, coffee, and cocoa. In
the realm of religion we hear of instant

healings. A young woman phones a prayer ministry and requests prayers for enough desires to describe a lifetime of attainment. As if she were giving a grocery list she asks impatiently, "How soon can I expect results?"

It doesn't take very long for most things to take place when the way is prepared for them. It is the getting ready that takes the time!

What It Takes

The black comedian describes in an interview the years of trial-and-error efforts in squalid bars and sleazy nightclubs that prepared him for his sensationally successful appearance in a late night television show which was to rocket him into opulence. Notwithstanding all the highly developed technology that turns out motor cars at such a fantastic rate, it has taken the skill of many inventive minds and patient efforts through the better part of a century to achieve such results. It is a long journey from the days of the Wright brothers and prophetic imaginings of a Jules Verne to bring us into the air age. And even as you read this you may become impatient with the time required for the reading. As this is being written one automotive company buys a double page of advertising in a leading weekly to advocate no-fault liability insurance, with each section of its reasoning headed "reading time, 25 seconds; reading time, 60 seconds; reading time, 35 seconds," lest the reader be turned off by the number of words.

What results, then, can you expect from your efforts to discipline thoughts, feelings, attitudes?

You will get immediate results, or indications that results are on the way, as soon as you open the way for them to appear.

Clear the way of doubt, fear, and other adverse notions that might clog the channel. Don't be like the timorous driver whose car barely made the grade of a steep hill. When finally it reached the summit, the driver turned to his wife and said, "I don't think we'd ever have made it, if I hadn't kept one foot on the brakes to keep her from rolling backward!" Prepare for the good you seek, in as many ways as you can think of, then relax and trust in the universal law of cause and effect, action and reaction, sowing and reaping, for the maximum right outcome.

Center your energies on causes. Resist the temptation to be unduly concerned with results. They will follow in natural order — and promptly.

After Its Kind

In the natural order, everything works from within outward. Results begin in the hidden realm of preparation. You plant a seed in the ground. You till the soil, you water it. It may seem as if nothing is happening. When you were a child, you may have been one who couldn't wait, couldn't believe that anything was happening because you couldn't *see* that it was happening. You stuck your fingers down into the moist earth and uncovered the tiny seed, perhaps already beginning to send a root downward, a shoot upward, but the shoot was not yet able to push through to the light.

Everything begins as an idea, a mental concept, a pattern. The pattern of the snowflake is inherent in water vapor. The pattern of the oak tree is in the acorn. The plant preexists in the seed. "First the blade, then the ear, then the full grain in the ear."

The pattern of your own life's fulfillment is in you as the pattern of the oak tree is in the acorn, the pattern of the snowflake in water vapor. *You always carry with you the thing you tend to seek outwardly.* There is an innate desire in all of us to follow that inward pattern even without realizing that there is a pattern. Desire is the blueprint of that pattern. Thought is your reading of the blueprint. Feeling activates the thought. Desire is prophetic of its own fulfillment. Universal Mind is the power. You are the director of that power. It will take whatever form you give it by the nature of your thoughts, feelings, words, actions.

"Everything brings forth after its kind."

Emerson startled many of his readers by asserting that the dice of God are always loaded. By this we take him to mean that the natural order of things is for each of us to become what from the beginning we were intended to be. It is hard to go against the natural order, made so to steer us back into line. The impossible is not demanded of us. We are equipped with inner resources to become in fact what we are in truth, to use the inward powers of creative, constructive thought and feeling to fulfill every good desire.

Prophets of old used to go apart from mundane activities periodically to renew their creative powers of mind. It is an example profitable in the present day when virtually everything of a material nature is emphasized. The things of the higher nature are seldom advertised. We must seek them out. The practical way is to take some time every day for the long view, the high view, of what we are and are to be; that we may become consciously that which we are eternally.

Meditation is the means of reawakening our latent forces. Any time is a good time for this. Having a regular time daily is most effective.

The temptation is to react with the assertion, "I don't have the time." It is more accurate to say that we don't *take* the time. Truly finding the time seems difficult at first, and possibly ineffectual. Only experience can demonstrate its value. A good place to start is to use the time while waiting to keep an appointment, or some other moments when the regular order of affairs is interrupted. As we become familiar with a way of procedure, we discover how relaxing and renewing it is. All through this book you will find affirmative statements that are like mental road maps, very helpful in getting us where we want to go. And results are not delayed. They are immediate.

Seven Steps to Take

Here are seven steps conducive to meditating in depth. There is nothing arbitrary about them. They have been tried, tested, and employed by people from time immemorial, way back before the advent of Jesus.

1. *Agreement.* Agree, accept, consent. Say of no good desire, "It is too good to be true." Accept the opposite concept. "Either the good as I see it, or what in God's sight is even better, shall become manifest." If you say that nothing can be done, that there is no answer for the problem, no help for your sense of need, then you are working against your own good, your own inner sense of guidance that prompts you to aspire to betterment. Dwell on the thought that there is help, that a good outcome is possible, that God wants you to find and rejoice in His blessing.

2. *Be Affirmative.* If God were to ask you, "What shall I do for thee?" what would your answer be? Avoid negation. Let not your thoughts and feelings center

on what you do not want. Sometimes it seems easier for us to think, "Well, I don't want thus-and-so," than to think what we really do want. But this attitude is not productive.

Dwell on the good as you conceive it to be, and let it be an open-ended good. Keep in mind that the good as we see it is seldom an ultimate. Good shall, in God's plan for us, be followed by greater good, "miracle shall follow miracle, and wonders never cease."

3. *The Right Start.* Count your blessings. Consider what you have to begin with. What are your talents? What have you accomplished that has been useful and recognized by others? "A journey of a thousand miles must be taken a step at a time," is the old Chinese saying. Don't dwell on the thousand miles, except in the thought that there can be good all along the way. Be willing, as we all must be, to start right where we are. "A man's gift maketh room for him," Solomon declared. The declaration is still valid. We might wish we could start somewhere else than where we are

— hopefully on a higher level — but there is real adventure in proving our way. To paraphrase John Burroughs,

> Asleep, awake, by night or day,
>   The good I seek is seeking me;
> No wind can drive my bark astray,
>   Nor change the tide of destiny.

4. *Preparation.* Let the picturing power of positive thinking prepare the way for greater attainment. See yourself physically strong, well, vigorous; mentally alert, enthusiastic; emotionally in dominion, filled with love and goodwill toward others, accepted and acceptable, appreciated and appreciative; spiritually at one with the Source of all being, whose intent is good and only good.

5. *Expectancy.* With your realization of God as your partner, all things will work, and are now working, together for good. "When thou art come in, shut the door"; that is, when you have attuned thought and feeling to the standard of right outcome, close the door of thought against failure. Say, *"I am positive*

against all that is beneath (unworthy of) me, receptive to all that is above." Or as James puts it, "If any of you lack wisdom, let him ask of God, that giveth to all men liberally. . . . But let him ask in faith, nothing wavering. For he that wavereth is like a wave of the sea driven with the wind and tossed" (James 1:5,6).

6. *Active Faith.* Write down any thoughts that come to you that will act out your faith in some objective form: a letter to write, a phone call to make, a program of self-improvement, some help you can render someone without thought of return.

7. *Give Thanks.* Give thanks for blessings of the past, those that are at hand, and those on the way. Be a good steward. Give, tithe of money and/or time, pass on a compliment, put some other good thought or feeling into circulation. Radiate a prayer of blessing to all of whom you think: people, places, things.

Mind is the master-power that molds
and makes,
The man is mind, and evermore
he takes
The tool of thought, and, shaping what
he wills,
Brings forth a thousand joys, a
thousand ills.
He thinks in secret and it comes
to pass;
Environment is but his
looking glass.

James Allen

How Long Will It Take?

How long before I will get results from my efforts at self-improvement? How soon can I become adept at meditation?

When you push the light button how soon does the light come on? Immediately, without delay. The amount of light is dependent upon a number of factors, but the reaction is immediate.

You will get immediate results for every good effort you make. The natural laws of life are impersonal and universal. No matter who you are, what you are, where you are, that action is inviolate, dependable, and accurate. As you sow, so you will reap. As you think, so you will become. No good effort is lost. No good action is without equal and opposite reaction. What you send out will come back to you in kind. You can be what you will to be.

Results are immediate. They are not always immediately apparent.

MEDITATION

I acclaim the goodness of God, of man, of the world. I agree, I accept, I consent to its manifestation in me, to me, through me.

I seek to accord what I want with what I need, in order to live at my highest best.

I think in terms of what I have, not what I lack. I remember that "a man's gift maketh room for him, and bringeth him before great men."

I make the most and the best of my God-given resources. They are my capital. I invest them in service.

I know that my faith is my fortune, and there is supply for every need.

I am an open channel through which the healing, prospering currents of God's life freely pour.

I give thanks that God is my instant, constant, and abundant supply of all good.

7
Don't Demand Difficulties

What is important to you is not so much the circumstances of your life as your attitude toward them.

The Frog in the Rut

The story is told of a frog who got in a deep rut in a road and couldn't get out. He tried and tried. All his frog friends came to advise and encourage him. His frog enemies came to taunt and gloat. But he was still in the rut. Night came on and all the frogs but him went wherever it is that frogs go at night. In the morning they foregathered to greet their rut-bound peer.

The rut was frogless.

Pretty soon its erstwhile captive came

hopping up, chipper as you please.

Somehow the others were a little disappointed.

"We thought you couldn't get out of the rut!" they exclaimed.

"Well, I couldn't, but a truck came along and I had to!"

In Extremis

Like the frog in the rut, some people never make any real progress until they are in such difficulties that they are forced to do something about them.

It is required that we learn and grow. It is not required that we suffer. But it is better to suffer and learn than not to learn at all — which is the greater suffering.

Better, then, to face issues affirming our personal adequacy, as Lloyd C. Douglas called it. We might put it, *"I am adequate and more than adequate for anything that is required of me. Nothing and no one can keep from me the good that God has for me."*

The Hidden Price Tag

True. But there is often a hidden, unrecognized factor in the matter of attaining the maximal degree of well-being in life. The key word is appreciation. Good things are naturally attracted to people who appreciate them and express their appreciation. "It's a joy to give you a rich gift, because you know and respect its value," and "I never know what to give you, because you seem to have everything, and what I can offer doesn't amount to much," are familiar reactions, in the first case to the person who makes his appreciation emphatically known, and in the second to one who either doesn't appreciate the gift (or the giver) or is remiss in making his appreciation known.

What Nobody Wants

Nobody wants to be taken for granted. The opera star may sing because of the financial compensation, but the enthusiastic response of the audience is what brings out the best in her. The accompanist too helps to bring out the best in her, and he too is sensitive to recognition and appreciation. The housewife is made happier when those she loves let her know how much they love the good meals she prepares, and her husband works better for an appreciative employer and for a family who let him know what a good husband and father they think he is. There's no question but what pets respond to praise and attention, and we're beginning to think there's more science than superstition to the old notion of gardeners talking to their plant pets.

We invite difficulties when we do even a good thing for a selfish reason.

We make gifts, we do favors, whose motive is to win love. We fail because a gift is not a gift, a favor is not a favor, if it expects or demands something in return. We can make people feel uncomfortable, embarrassed, or annoyed by such gifts. *We can make people hate us. We must win their love.* If we do things whose end is love, it is indeed the end of love. What we do because love is the cause of doing attracts its own gracious ends, and its own willing channels. As it is impossible to act from wrong or mistaken motives without undesirable results, so it is equally impossible to act simply, honestly, purely, and unselfishly without good results.

On the Right Side

These things should be self-evident, yet don't we all know of people who demand difficulties in life, who in one way or another are making things harder on themselves — and others — than is needful? In one way or another they all come under one general category. They are those who take a "downbeat" attitude toward life, who fail to realize that despite the many problems that beset us, the balance in life is on the "upbeat" side. Happy homes, well-adjusted children, law-abiding citizens do not make headlines in the news media.

We are justified in feeling concern

about crime, drugs, ecology, and other problems. Be concerned but not overwhelmed. Put your trust in right outcomes. There are preponderantly more "rights" than "wrongs." Don't demand more difficulties than there actually are.

Losers

We demand difficulties when we pretend to be something we are not. A mature woman with a light but lovely singing voice was romantically attracted to men much younger than herself. One young man especially attracted her, but he seemed oblivious to her efforts to arouse his interest. She pictured how happy she could be, what a handsome couple they would be, if only she were his age. She decided that she would diet and have a face-lift. She disappeared from the scene for awhile. When she returned she did indeed appear much younger. Her figure was slender, her voice was charming, her appearance that of a young woman. The young man she had set her heart upon responded to her transformed appearance. They married. But it did not work out, for while she appeared to be young, she was not young at heart. She found her husband to be handsome but dull. The things he and his young friends talked about were not interesting to her. Their youthful zest for physical exercise was exhausting. In turn, her husband found her to be possessive, opinionated, patronizing.

A young bank teller often sent in "lucky numbers" to a publishing house that used the enticement of miraculous winnings as a means of getting subscriptions to a book club. Miraculously he won a sum of $40,000. It was equal to several years' salary. He had never had so much money of his own in his possession. He was drawn into get-rich-quick schemes that were practically invented for people like him. In a short while the windfall was gone, and he was out of a job.

He had been happy in his teller's job, but the sudden exposure to a different scale of living made the job seem tedious by comparison. He became a kind of con man himself, skirting the edge of entanglement with the law, an unhappy, disoriented man.

The Organizer

We demand difficulties when we try to cut corners, skirt the law, violate traffic rules.

I used to know a racketeering undertaker named Joe. A young friend of mine had committed suicide over a love affair. I was involved in the memorial service. Following it, the handsome young undertaker sought me out, and began asking some unusually personal questions. Where had I gone to school? How did I learn to speak in public? Where did I get my clothes? What club did I belong to?

He had an arrangement with the county coroner by which many coroner's cases, as they were called, were turned over to him for burial. He had become affluent, and the combination of affluence and good looks had given him a certain entree into an element of society that was foreign to him.

Invited to social gatherings he encountered a communication gap. The people he met used terms that were unfamiliar to him, talked on subjects and about places that were strange to him. ''I sent my parents on a trip to Europe. I thought that when they came back they could tell me about it. They couldn't tell me anything!'' he deplored.

My heart went out to the man. ''He wants to improve himself. He wants to be what he thinks of as a gentleman,'' I thought. ''Maybe I can help him.'' But his next words were disillusioning. ''You know there's a smaller city about fifty miles from here that is not organized. I could go in there, offer 'protection' to the main street merchants, and set up a nice little rake-off for myself!''

He didn't really want to be a ''gentleman.'' He just wanted people to think he was. My profession took me to another city halfway across the country. I often wondered what had befallen Joe.

Had he "organized" a town he could dominate, or had he become (belatedly) a gentleman? It was some years before I had occasion to revisit the city where I had known Joe. "Whatever has become of him?" I asked a mortician. "Oh, he was liquidated," was the answer. "It evidently was a gang killing. His body was found in an alley, full of lead.

Achieving Balance

We demand difficulties when we fail to achieve or work toward a balance between the different aspects of our human nature. Paul saw them as two, the physical and the spiritual, and asserted that the two must be reconciled in one body. One of our present-day problems is that we have discovered a third aspect of our nature, the mind or intellect. This is a great discovery which could make it a kind of catalyst, uniting the other two, but often has been allowed to appear more like a two-edged sword that would cleave them asunder.

Booth Tarkington told the story of a man whose whole life was so centered on the fulfillment and gratification of his physical nature that when he died and went into another dimension it was like being in the hell that the old-fashioned preachers knew so much about, because he still had all the desires of his physical nature, but no physical body through which to gratify them. In a world of mind and soul he was alone, isolated, bereft.

Every increase in knowledge demands wisdom, but it broadens man's horizon and opens vistas of expansion and fulfillment.

We lose something for everything we gain, but the loss too is gain. We lose angels that archangels may replace them, we lose the anthropomorphic God of the earth-centered age for the universal God of the space age. Paul's assertion, "I die daily," which must have seemed fantastic hyperbole to his contemporaries is now seen to be almost literally true. Advance in human thought and discovery is so rapid in recent years that scientific books are largely obsolete before they come off the printing presses.

Difficulties Dominated

Most everyone I know is seeking some way of life in which there are no problems. But the only place I know in which there are no problems — and I am sure someone must have said this before me — is in the cemetery. Outside the cemetery there are two kinds of problems, and a great difference between them.

There are the problems incident to growth, and there are the problems involved in resistance to growth. I am reminded of Plato's story of the man who escaped from an underground cavern. He groped his way by a winding stair into the upper world, and was like one bemused and blind. People called him an idiot. But he was a divine idiot, because the blindness in him was not that of deepening darkness but of growing light.

If we are growing there are sure to be problems of growth. These are wholesome problems, even though sometimes difficult. To take the attitude that there are answers for them, and that by the grace of God we can find the answers, transforms the challenge of the unanswered problems into an adventure of discovery; sometimes even of *self-*discovery. Life is always unfinished business. There is always a hill beyond a hill beyond a hill. Even perfection itself is not static but an evolvement, what Emerson called "the flying perfect." We think, "When I have reached such a point in attainment, I will be content . . . when the children are through school . . . when the mortgage is paid . . . when I can retire." Fortunately this is not so. Nothing in this world is changeless but change.

Insufferable Problems

The problems of rejecting growth are the insufferable ones, made so by the insistence of their victims that life must conform to their established life patterns.

For past generations it is conceivable that this kind of problem was not so difficult as it is in the present. Changes were more gradual. The horse-and-buggy period gave way slowly to railways and motor cars. But the change from surface transportation to aerial transportation was faster, and kept growing more so. The days of stage plays and vaudeville gave way gradually to silent motion pictures, nickelodeons, to Radio City Music Hall, and both in turn diminished before the hypnotic allure of the little domestic screen of television. The old morality is still wrestling with the *new* morality that seems almost like *no* morality.

The pace of progress is more rapid than at any other known time in history. Whereas in our grandparents' day, or at most in our great-grandparents' day, the changes in the mores and manners, the scientific, cultural, and religious progress were so gradual that they demanded very little mental or physical adjustment in an average lifetime, changes have radically accelerated. Like a snowball rolling down a steep hillside, growing larger and moving faster and faster, world changes have taken on the aspect of an avalanche that threatens accustomed values and direction.

As in most everything, the threatening aspect of things and the problems involved are discerned before the possible benefits and solutions appears.

Prophets of Doom

The most highly educated and articulate authorities of the present are the most pessimistic about our future. "We are faced by insuperable problems!" The senior citizens will remark that there were insuperable problems in their day, too; the proliferation of disease would wipe out humanity within twenty-five years. Probably what saved humanity of that era was that the news of impending doom did not reach enough people to cause universal despair.

Problems are a part of the human condition. Even Adam, when he was escorting Eve out of Eden, probably turned to her and said, "Well, dear, these are troubled times you know!" Yes, problems are part of the human condition, but only a part and the lesser part at that.

Individually, we die a little and are born a little with every breath we draw, for truly "the body, though it be one, has many members," and that doesn't mean simply hands, feet, and so on, but that the cells and atoms of the body in which we dwell are continually being born, living their little life-span and being replaced by others, all so much within the outward form of the body as we know it, that for the most part we are unaware of the twin miracles of death and birth by which we live.

Mentally perhaps it is a little more obvious to us that we die to many old forms of thought, and are born to new and better ones.

And if we live deeply as well as long, we are in the process of discovering that "man does not live by bread alone," or even by his intellect, but by what seems to be an impregnation by a super-mind, a mind that is less of thought and more of feeling, an extension of the faculties, or the awakening of faculties not previously recognized. The dawning may come as quietly as the wafting of thistledown upon the air, or in the dramatic manner that Thomas Moore described in *Lalla Rookh:*

And from the lips of Truth
    one mighty breath
Shall like a whirlwind scatter
    in its breeze
That whole dark pile of
    human mockeries; —
Then shall the reign of mind
    commence on earth,
And starting fresh as from
    a second birth,
Man in the sunshine of the world's
    new spring
Shall walk transparent like some
    holy thing!

MEDITATION

I am open, receptive, responsive to guidance and direction, and to correction if need be. I meet life's issues as they arise. I do not run away from challenges, but transform them into opportunities by calling upon the untried capacities which await my discovery. I do not pretend to be something I am not, but seek instead to be what in God's sight I am in truth, and what I am becoming in fact, by my recognition of and response to His nature within me. I do not take other people nor my own good fortune for granted! I strive to be a good appreciator. I give thanks for the place where I live, for a wholesome body, a sane mind, a loving heart, for work to do, and ability to do it, for relaxation and rest at the close of the day.

8
Making Friends With Life

There is a bridge, whereof the span
Is rooted in the heart of man.

Gilbert Thomas

Life Is Good

In order to attain to the good life we have
to learn that life is good.

We have to know that people are good
(often better than they believe
themselves to be, an ignorance that often
causes them and others much trouble);
that the universal order of things is good
and essentially the way it should be; that
life and people are vastly interesting,
have much to reveal to us, much to teach
us and to bring enrichment to our
personal world.

Don't be afraid of people. Don't be afraid of life. They have much to give us, but we have to be receptive.

Some people are like the late Will Rogers, who "never met a stranger" nor "a man he didn't like." Most of us are not that self-confident or that outgoing. I am not, quite. For instance, speaking in public was one of the most difficult things I ever had to do. Why then did I persist in it? Because I had a teacher who had faith in my ability to overcome this fear. He believed that the only way to overcome a fear is to face it, and by many means and over quite a period of time he instilled this belief into me. With regard to public speaking he would not let me give up. He would coax and plead and praise and goad me, and even rage against me, but he would not let me go.

I was afraid of strangers, afraid of the sound of my voice, afraid of speaking before even a small group of friends. I was even more afraid of larger groups, such as a Sunday morning congregation. He said this was false pride, a form of egotism. I thought it was an act of mercy to the congregation. Maybe it was something of both. At the present stage of my life, I feel an empathy with the people in the pews. The larger the crowd the better I do. I sometimes tell my congregation that I have an allergy that only they can cure. *I am allergic to empty seats!* Emmet Fox and I used to speculate on what attracted crowds to a speaker. He asserted that it was what he called "crowd consciousness." He said that he prayed about this a lot. I observed that he also worked to improve his message and delivery.

To Overcome Fear

How do you overcome fear of people, singly or in groups?

By getting to know them. By having the grace — and maybe the good sense — to realize quite simply that people are people, regardless of their status in life, their racial or religious background, their erudition. As a very young minister I spent a lot of time trying to impress people with what I knew. I talked about the most abstruse subjects I could devise. Without realizing it until much later, I was actually trying to impress myself, to attain self-confidence, to gain the assurance that I could attract and hold people's attention. (I had to learn that the only legitimate reason for being a minister was *to minister*, to help people.)

A Key to Empathy

Then one day I strayed from my announced topic, "The Fourth Dimension," and rambled or stumbled into talking of some problems that were very close to my heart and to simple human needs. For the first time, I believe, I then established a real rapport with the congregation. This was attested by their comments at the close of the meeting, when they did not merely say, "I enjoyed the sermon," but a heartier, "You really hit home this morning," or "That talk was just for me."

Somewhat to my embarrassment I have discovered that other speakers are often as puzzled as I am about what makes people listen to me. I came upon a little huddled group of ministers at a religious convention one time. As I approached, their animated conversation came to an abrupt stop. One of their number broke the strained silence:

"We were just talking about you," he remarked.

"That's interesting. What did you say?"

"We were speculating on what it is about you that attracts crowds of people."

"That has puzzled a lot of people," I confessed.

"I think I know the answer," the bold one responded.

"Okay, what do you think it is?" I pressed.

"You'd be the last to claim that you are an orator. I think it is because you love people," he said quietly.

I hope that that has a lot to do with it, but to put it quiet simply, I think that the main thing is that I talk about things that I myself are interested in, enthusiastic about, working on; and that this strikes a responsive chord in others. Talking about things that people maybe *should* be interested in may be a nod to the proprieties of ministerial behavior. But when I talk about the problems and aspirations that are common to us all in this day of changing standards, ecology, young people's rejection (yet dependency upon) the establishment and their assertion of sexual freedom, requests for copies of sermons double.

Why? Because "every man is the leading character in his own life's drama," as Florence Scovil Schinn says.

What Everyone Needs

Let a man's name appear in a listing of a hundred, or even on a page of newsprint. His eyes will pick it out. Let his name be spoken amid the babble of a dozen voices raised in conversation, his ears will detect it even though he had a hearing loss. Second only to the sight and sound of his name is his response to the mention of personal problems, challenges, and aspirations with which he identifies. A feeling for people as individuals surpasses the gifts of oratory in winning the interest and response of assemblies large or small, in all walks of life. I once heard a silver-haired reconteuse convulse a Rotarian luncheon group by describing the hero in a fable she was telling, when she said of the hero he devoted his life to a service to others. "He looked," she asserted, "very much like the white-haired gentleman seated near the end of the table," as she pointed. Unbeknown to her he happened to be a prominent mortician. On another occasion, she also got a similar reaction telling a children's group about a youthful prince and princess. "The prince looked like this young man with freckles and red hair," and of the princess, "Her gown was the color of this little girl's rose-colored dress, and her hair was as black as that of the little girl in the corner."

Jesus was a master of this ageless psychology, an uncontrived and spontaneous empathy with people. He called Zacchaeus by name and bade him come down out of the sycamore tree into which he had climbed in order to see the Master. "I'm coming to sup with you," he announced. And of Nathanael Bar-Tolemai, "I saw you under that fig tree," and to the fishermen who were to become His apostles, "Come ye after me, and I will make you to become fishers of men!" He expounded wisdom in terms of the agrarians He was addressing; spoke of birds and their nests, foxes and their holes, wine and wineskins, sower and seed, sheep and their shepherd, treasures hidden in a field. "Without a parable spake he naught to them," Matthew tells us.

Be yourself, hopefully your best self. Relate to others. Communicate. You cannot be just like anyone else, nor should you try, except to remember that down underneath the little foibles and eccentricities, the superficial differences that sometimes make real communication challenging, we are all very much alike in our basic needs and desires. "One loving heart can set another heart on fire," to paraphrase St. Augustine.

The Generation Gap

Even the generation gap is probably only one phase of the communication gap. Taylor Caldwell built a whole book around a very simple concept; a chapel to which troubled people could go and voice their sense of need to an unseen Listener. They never saw the Listener who was hidden from their sight. They heard no outward voice except their own, yet they found answers to their perplexities, even relief and pardon. How general is this sense of need is attested by the popularity of a radio program offering a thought for the day, or dial-a-prayer telephone recorded messages. A letter comes to me from such a listener, who adds a postscript. "I think you have a sense of humor. Have you heard about the man 'who never got no respect,' and was so unlucky that when he phoned dial-a-prayer it hung up

119

on him!"

A modern practical psychologist confesses that in his practice he seldom gives advice. He simply listens, really listens, and merely asks a pertinent question now and then, though he might admit that knowing the right questions is important. The patients' most frequent comment as they leave is, "Oh, doctor, you've helped me so much!" A sympathetic listener helps them find the needed answer from their own innate wisdom.

In making friends with life, do you feel that it is an intrusion on the privacy of someone you are meeting for the first time to ask him what kind of work he does, where he lives, what his hobbies are? Being asked such questions, are you repelled? After the first shock in finding that someone really seems interested, does it not open possible areas of communication, possible friendship? Seldom is such implied interest taken amiss. For "every man is the leading character in his own life's drama."

The Most Helpful Words

The need to communicate meaningfully is very real. We all want to be better understood. The corollary to this need is the need to be understanding of others, their interests, their challenges, their goals. A doctor friend of mine declares that the two most helpful words in the language are "I understand."

Americans travelling in foreign countries always seem to expect people to understand English, and in most of the great cities and tourist centers many people do. But if you get off the beaten track you may find it quite otherwise. A friendly attitude, smiles, and gestures will go a long way in overcoming the communication gap. The little tourists' phrase books often help too, although those I've found seemed to be planned for visitors travelling by train whereas most of us have been airborne, and are being car borne or bus borne and the words don't fit. At home we are often amused at foreigners' efforts to master the intricacies of English. When we are abroad we find that a sincere effort to try out a phrase or two of the native tongue is never ridiculed, almost always treated with appreciation and as a compliment. Perhaps you remember the late President Kennedy's effort at greeting Berliners in German? And I recall a visit to Oberammergau to see the Passion Play in its tercentary season, having breakfast in the village doctor's home. My fellow guests were a Dutch honeymooning couple, two Austrian priests, and three Swedish-Americans. By bits and pieces, with the aid of fragmentary phrases and pantomime, amazingly self-consciousness waned, and a jovial feeling of fellowship and communion was established.

How Not to Like Others

The only way really not to like people is not to let them get close enough or familiar enough to know them. Even then you may not — almost surely will not —

like everything about them, everything they do. But you will tend to reach beyond *where* they are in attainment, and how much or little you have in common with them, to *what* they are, and to the greatest thing we all have in common: that "now are we the children of God, and it does not yet appear what we shall be."

That we should love all persons equally well strains credulity. There are some with whom we feel a deep bond of kinship at a first meeting. We welcome them like old friends returned. There are others whom we may seem to have known most of a lifetime yet find in some crucial experience that we have not really known at all.

The Healer Attitude

How should, or how can, we reconcile such disparities? You might find what I call "the healer attitude" helpful. If someone is in trouble and he asks you to pray for him, you are likely to discover that any antagonistic or critical attitude you may have entertained about him begins to modify and disappear. You find yourself on the defensive for him, wanting to see the good in him, wanting others to see him as you do. You and the troubled one may never become bosom pals, but you will be freeing him, in your thought, from his own sense of limitation and thereby freeing yourself from the tendency to pass judgment where it is not demanded.

Universal Love

Try thinking in a friendly way of the forces of nature as well as of people. Primitive man lived in fear of the elements. He personified these forces as deities whose favors must be won and whose angers must be apppeased by offerings and sacrifices. Even within the last century the seas were considered as barriers separating peoples and continents. The force of gravity, it was thought, would hold man down to earth, making flying impractical if not impossible. Electricity was a force that rent the skies in raging storms, an alien power that imperilled life and limb. But James Watt discovered the power of steam by observing the clicking lid of a teakettle, and Fulton invented a steam engine to propel a boat. Soon the rivers and oceans became lanes of commerce. Franklin sent up a kite that captured lightning and contained it in a bottle, and men began to learn the ways that electricity operates, thereby making vast cities, vast industries possible. The Wright brothers and others experimented with aerial flight and learned among many other things that if it weren't for the force of gravity, once man had left the earth he would have a very hard time getting back. Einstein and others ushered in the atomic age. Darwin brought a scientific approach to the origin of the species. With almost sudden impact — for a century is a brief time in relation to the age of the earth on which man lives, and the time since he first appeared upon it — from every direction, scientific, religious, philosophical, cultural, came the intimations that everything is related. And a century before Darwin and the present age of science, the poet Alexander Pope proclaimed:

All are but parts of one
   stupendous whole,
Whose body Nature is, and God
   the Soul.

Nature everywhere signals to us that we are a part of it, and it is a part of us; that movement, growth, change are inescapable characteristics of the universal life force; that probably nothing in the universe is completely inanimate; every stone is a mass of whirling motion about tiny centers of electric energy, tiny points of light. Life energy is protean in character, but is a continuum in which birth and death are but incidents. It manifests in patterns that correctly express the idea characterizing its nature.

Midway between the infinitely small and the infinitely large is man, the epitome of all that is beneath him, the prophecy of all that is to be.

What a piece of work is a man! how noble in reason! how infinite in faculty! in form and moving how express and admirable! in action how like an angel! in apprehension how like a god!

Hamlet, act II, sc. ii

MEDITATION

I give thanks for the wonderful world in which we live; for the good green earth, for the sun by day and the moon by night, and the steadfast stars; for shade on sunny days, and refreshing coolness following rain; for the surging energies of fire and air, of earth and sea.

I am grateful for the manifold friendly forms of life in the world around me, for rocks and trees and grass, for hills and valleys and mountains and seas, for animals and birds, for fish and the seas and lakes and streams in which they swim, for shrubs and vines and flowers whose form and scent and color add beauty to my days.

I am grateful for all friendly humanity, for those with whom I have rapport, and for those others who teach me as they dispute the passage with me.

And I'm grateful most of all for the God who made us all.

9
If You Don't Like Yourself — And If You Do

I will not let my grievous past with
   vain regrets torment me —
I can't help feeling that my acts don't
   really represent me.

Rebecca McCann

A False Blow

"You may be God to everybody else around here, but before I leave this place, I want you to know that you are not God to me!" a young woman who worked in the advertising department of an organization I once served, declared.

"That's a great blow to me," I responded. And before the words were out of my mouth I realized that that probably was the worst thing I could have said. I should have tried to understand why she had said it, and what I might do to help her.

I tried to redeem the error as I saw she was about to turn and leave my office. "Don't go yet. I'm not God to me either and I need all the help I can get to try to measure up to the job I'm trying to do." She sat down opposite me while I tried to think how to redeem the error my erratic sense of humor had prompted.

What she didn't know was that I had been going through a challenging time, in which something that I thought was a valuable and unselfish project had been rejected. Smarting from defeat and the feeling that I was not appreciated, I had slipped into the meditation chapel that was available to employees, and became lost in thoughts of self-justification. These gave way to a kind of numbness, followed by a more rational feeling of wishing that I could have thought, and hoped I still could think, of some better way to present my cherished ambition. I felt a touch on my arm, and found that a man had come in quietly and was sitting beside me.

"Is something troubling you?" he asked.

"I'm walking on my heart!" I exclaimed.

"Then if I can be the first to tell you all the good things I've observed about you I'll feel that it is a special privilege."

How wonderfully he ministered to my battered ego!

So that was how I could say with abandon, "That's a great blow to me!"

But what had I done to my derogator?

"Gwenn, you're not God to me, either. But you're doing a good job and if I haven't let you know I think so, it's time and past time that I did. What I think about you may not be important to you, but you are important to the success of the work we're both interested in, and unless there is something greater that you are going to by leaving here, I hope you'll stay."

She didn't stay, but at least we parted with better feelings on both sides than when she had entered, or sort of burst into, my office. Appreciation can surely inspire greater efforts at productivity, but appreciation of itself isn't really worth enough. It's like frosting on a cake, a kind of serendipity.

A Graver Error

I became aware of another mistake I had made, a greater one by far than saying, "That's a great blow to me." The greater mistake which Gwenn's sarcastic remark brought unpleasantly to my recognition was that not everybody liked me, and that it was quite possible that though I thought of myself as a likeable person, and supposed that I really wanted to be likeable, the term is a variable, with different meanings to every individual, so that whatever I might do most surely would not please everybody. A budding politician was recently quoted, following his first (and unsuccessful) campaign: "I don't think I have the intestinal fortitude to take the criticism, innuendoes, outright lies, and slander that running for office involves — not to mention the expense, the time, and the uncertainties involved in even one campaign."

Can You Accept Criticism?

In various degrees every one in public life is faced by these things. Much later than the episode with Gwenn my career took me to Southern California where I became acquainted with some of the brighter and dimmer luminaries of the stage and screen. A stage star was commenting on the, to her, ghastly experience of seeing the details of her not unattractive and very expressive face magnified to gargantuan proportions, which made every detail of her appearance more intimately viewed than sitting face to face with someone.

She had recently appeared in a stage role which was caustically panned by the critics, but became a tremendous success with the public. I asked her what her reaction was to such criticism.

"Of course it is hard to take. They have a right to their opinion, and they earn their living by the comments they make. It appears that the more caustic they are the more readers they have. But there is more fury than light in what they write. The coach I have worked with, and the director, are the ones I count on to supplement whatever natural and acquired gifts I have. I suspect that anyone in public life has his detractors no matter how capable or dedicated he may be. Look at what they did to Jesus Christ!''

Dorothy Canfield tells, in an article in *The Christian Century* magazine, about her experience in speaking before a group of teen-aged girls. One of them asked how she reacted to criticism of her novels. When she mentioned that no doubt they had found that not all their acquaintances liked them, she observed an expression of shocked dismay on their faces. Apparently they were not prepared for such a thought. Perhaps the turning point from immaturity (at any age) to true maturity comes when we can accept that fact of life with equanimity.

I know a lady minister who went to a hard job — and being a lady minister must be a hard job to begin with! She tells me that she entered the office of her new charge unannounced. When she told the only person present, a woman who happened to be a member of the board filling in at the receptionist's desk, who she was, the greeting she got was, "There's one thing I want you to get straight right at the beginning. I didn't vote for you, I don't like women ministers to begin with, and I hope you will be replaced."

"Well, I see that we have a couple of things in common and that is a good start. First, you say what you think without evasion, and so do I. But even more important is that I love this church, and I know you do, for you've given years of dedicated service to it. I believe we both love it enough so that we can reach beyond personalities toward service to something more important."

They shook hands on it and worked at it.

In Disguise

I have heard a lot about superiority and inferiority complexes. Mostly the people who seem to have a superiority complex impress me as suffering from a disguised inferiority complex. They overcompensate. They tend either to treat newcomers to their circle like intruders or else "take over" too effusively. They are too unsure of themselves just to be natural. In argument or disagreement they tend to state their opinions as if they were incontrovertible fact. They tend to say "I think" rather than "Do you think . . . ?" They incline to "lord it over others," and when something in which they are involved doesn't turn out well, try to shift the blame.

As the Blame Shifts

People who don't like themselves find it difficult to like and trust others; if others seem reserved it must be because they are hiding something; if they are outgoing they are show-offs. Such an attitude is hard on themselves and on others with whom they are associated. They sense this, but not their own culpability. It is fate, or not knowing the right people, or — reflecting the mores of the times — karma or numerology or their astrological configuration. Any or all of these concepts might have a part, I say (not without some doubt), but over three hundred years ago Shakespeare had his own trenchant way of dealing with such efforts to evade responsibility, when he had Cassius say to Brutus: "The fault, dear Brutus, is not in our stars, / But in ourselves, that we are underlings."

If You Really Like —

If we don't like ourselves reasonably well, it is virtually impossible to like others very much. I say reasonably well, because too much is arrogance, conceit; too little is as unfair as it makes us be toward others. We do not want to be like the man whom two friends — not *his* friends I might say — were discussing:

"Despite his other faults, he is a modest man."

"— And has so much to be modest about!"

Perhaps it is not within reason for us to like all persons equally. We tend to form snap judgments, often subject to change as mysteriously as they are formed. "I never liked a man named Oscar," one friend of mine remarks. "I've always liked every girl I've known who was named Ruth," declares another. "His form and face, his manly grace, are not the type that you would find in a statue," the song says of "just my Bill' in *Showboat*. Unaccountably, too, we sometimes inwardly reject a person who seems on all accounts to merit acceptance. Two hundred years ago an irreverent student, Tom Brown, in his classroom at Oxford wrote a few lines of doggerel that have become something of a classic:

I do not like thee, Doctor Fell.
The reason why I cannot tell;
But this alone I know full well,
I do not like thee, Doctor Fell.

Most readers who have a superlative degree of self-approval will not have read this far in this slender volume. They will have sought other channels of acceptance and approval. Most of us probably underestimate ourselves. What we have attained by way of overcoming and self-mastery we are inclined to accept for whatever it is worth, and much, possibly too much, of our attention is centered on further heights to climb, further goals to reach. Like Paul, who was quite an overcomer, we are likely to agree: "I am still not all I should be but I am bringing all my energies to bear on this one thing; forgetting the past and looking forward to what lies ahead, I strain to reach the end of the race and receive the prize for which God is calling us," and "I have fought a good fight, I have finished my course, I have kept the faith."

Not with resignation but with trust we

come to see that

> Heaven is not reached at a single bound;
> But we build the ladder by which
>   we rise
> From the lowly earth to the
>   vaulted skies,
> And we mount to its summit round
>   by round.
>
> Josiah Gilbert Holland

There is a great illusion that we must strive to overcome: it is the notion that all of happiness consists in reaching goals, in finding perfect attainment in a perfect world of perfect people. We probably do not even know what perfection is. Emerson speaks of "the flying perfect." Certainly perfection is not static, but ever flowing, ever expanding, ever evolving, at least so far as this plane of existence is concerned. The greatest achievements we make on the human plane pall as time goes on. Nothing is absolute, nothing is final.

Acceptance

Every ending evolves into a new beginning. The maximum contentment, joy, and sense of fulfillment is in having a sense of values and a sense of direction, and accepting the goodness of life and people; the goodness that is latent in ourselves. Acceptance is a key word. Accept yourself. Accept the day that is at hand. "Each moment . . . has its own beauty . . . a picture which was never seen before and which shall never be seen again." Accept people, accept the infinite variety of life's manifestation. Accept change, the surge and flow of time and life. Accept the fact that only the good is enduringly true, all else "comes to pass." Let it pass. Suffer it to be so. Affirm, "I am in stride with the upward, progressive movement of life, and the mark of success is upon me."

MEDITATION

Help me, O Lord, to be wiser than my years, stronger than my fears, humble in whatever knowledge and learning I have attained, tolerant toward the foibles of others as I would have them be of mine. Let me not bog down in a miasma of self-pity over a sense of being misunderstood or ill-treated, nor self-inflated over some small worldly attainment that seems big to me because it is mine.

Grant me the long view to put temporal things in proper perspective, the short view which helps to focus my energies in the present, the high view that overlooks shortcomings in others and myself, and a sense of humor that enables me to give a light touch to things that look too big when approached with solemnity.

Help me, in the midst of things temporal, not to lose sight of things eternal; of Thee, most of all.

10
Preparing For Prosperity

If you write a better book, or preach a better sermon, or build a better mousetrap than your neighbor, the world will make a beaten path to your door.

"The Right Button"

"If you push the right button the light will come on," I've written elsewhere. The laws of being are no respecters of persons. They work the same for everybody. The results are not uniform because individuals are not uniform in the way they understand and conform to these laws. No matter who you are, where you are, what you have done or failed to do in the past, the law works.

The law of prosperity is that of action and reaction, sowing and reaping, giving and receiving. *You cannot even get another breath until you give the one you have!* Giving comes first.

What about our natural heritage of the gifts of God and nature? Where does giving fit to these? You have to give your attention, your interest, your understanding, your response. Until then you are like the youngster who found a diamond and didn't know it. To him it was only a piece of glass, and pretty crude glass at that, fit only to load a slingshot.

Eight Proven Steps

There are eight proven steps in attainment revealed in an Old Testament story in II Kings 4:1 - 7. If you follow them faithfully, they will lead to better health and prosperity. The law of attainment applies equally both ways, for health might be considered as prosperity of the physical organism, and prosperity as health in finances and affairs. The story in II Kings is the account of the widow, the prophet, and the cruse of oil. It is important enough to form the pattern of a book. Briefly the eight steps are:

1. Agreement

"There cried a certain woman . . . unto Elisha." As long as you say there is no help, no way of overcoming some problem or limitation, you are closing the door against a good outcome. It is your decree, and as we read in the book of Job, "Thou shalt also decree a thing, and it shall be established unto thee." The first little ray of light appears on an otherwise dark horizon when you begin to think that just maybe, possibly, perhaps there is hope of a good outcome. Agree, consent, accept the idea that a good result is possible.

One reason why many prayers are not answered is not that God wills it so, but that the person praying is centering his thoughts, feelings, energies on the wrong thing. He is concentrating on his troubles instead of on the Creative Principle that can help him out of his troubles. It is not practical to center our thoughts on darkness. Concentrate rather on light that dispels darkness.

2. Definite Desire

"What shall I do for thee?" What you want, not what you lack, should be the focus of attention. Sometimes it seems easier to define what we do not want than what we do want, especially when something we don't want is very much manifest in our life and world, and a replacement by something more nearly to the heart's desire is only a vague ephemeral dream. Centering on lack, you are in effect seeking to go *from* something. Centering on attainment, you are going *toward* something.

"Multitudes, multitudes in the valley of decision," cried Joel; and multitudes there are today; people seeking a way out of some situation, some human relationship, some disagreeable task. Often they feel that if only they had a better helpmeet, a different employer, a different vocation, a different area in which to live, they would be happier, more prosperous, in better health.

Sometimes, indeed, any combination of these notions may be indicated. More often it is better to reexamine the situation where we are. Unless there is a causative change of thought, feeling, and attitude, we are likely to find that no matter how much people and things around us may be changed, their impact on us will not be very different. Have we made the most and best of things-as-they-are? Have we learned all we can, taught all we can, given all that we can? Unless and until then, there is something holding us to the present. We have to grow out of it, instead of go out of it. It's like the youth in Belasco's *The Return of Peter Grimm,* who was disappointed in love and wanted to leave Holland, the scene of the play, and come to America. Peter tells him, "Go out into the garden and dig up the tulip bulbs. You can change your mind here just as well as in America."

3. Concentration

"What hast thou?" Waste none of your creative energy on negations, obstacles, difficulties. Someone has said you cannot solve a problem so long as you are in it. It is useless to belabor the point that it may well be that the problem may be in you instead of your being in it. How to change it? Try perspective. View it as "a" problem, not as "your" problem. Someone comes to you with such a problem. What would you tell him to do? What possible solutions can you see? Or how can you find one if none is obvious? Can you take the attitude that *"there are no unsolvable problems, no impossible situations, no impassable obstacles, no insurmountable barriers, no incurable diseases. God is a/my help in every need, and in the need of this moment"*?

Out of the possible answers to the need, which one can you best live with?

4. Preparation

"Borrow thee vessels." What can you do to make way for the good you seek? "If you pray for rain, carry an umbrella." Perhaps opportunity seeks the man as much as the man seeks opportunity; but just to be on the safe side, do something that you know by experience always tends to work out, as persistently as water seeks channels that will take it to the sea. Be prepared. Preparedness attracts opportunity as the magnet draws the steel. Abraham Lincoln is reputed to have said, "I will study and prepare, and some day my opportunity will come!"

A youth aspired to a writing career and took as many courses as he could afford toward such a goal. Family misfortunes necessitated that he interrupt his formal education and get a job that would augment the family income. He saw an advertisement in the want ads of the daily paper for an apprentice artist in a commercial engraving house. Having a slight skill he applied and got the job. He not only learned to draw acceptably, but also learned about other aspects of the craft, particularly the various methods of reproducing photographs, line and wash drawings, and four-color process engraving. This became engrossing to him, but seemingly had no relation to what he wanted to do with his life, until eleven years later when he was offered the editorship of an illustrated magazine. A time of necessity had led him into an unplanned preparation for a position that was eleven years away in the future.

Apparently such unpremeditated preparation plays a large part in the careers of many people. Two famous writers started out their careers as physicians, as did two world-renowned musicians. A motion picture star becomes a nun, another becomes a clergyman; so that it is as if a higher self is active behind the scenes, awaiting his appearance on the stage of life. It took Alexander Pope to phrase it:

All nature is but art unknown to thee,
All chance, direction which thou
   canst not see.

Looking backward this often seems clear, but the power of any life lies in its expectancy. Expect the good, even in unexpected ways. Claim that good and press the claim.

5. Vision

"Shut the door." "A picture," according to the ancient Chinese, "is worth ten thousand words." As many times as I had read the story of Moses climbing Mount Sinai, it never was so graphic as when, in the motion picture, *Green Pastures,* I saw the simulated figure of the aged prophet toiling his way upward, step by step, to the summit, where he saw stretched before him the Promised Land of his dreams. "Your old men shall dream dreams, your young men shall see visions," we quote from Joel again.

Word pictures can be effective as every reader of fiction knows, but visual pictures are more effective. Some people have found that making a "treasure map" of things hoped for is a graphic reminder, an incentive to pursue the gleam. Cut out pictures and words that illustrate objectives. Paste them on a large sheet of paper or cardboard. Place them where you will see them often. Change them as vision grows.

Is the vision getting clearer? The sense

of values, the sense of direction? Then, "when thou art come in . . . shut the door." In other words when you get a clear vision of what you seek and how to find it, shut the door of your mind and imagination against failure. Act as if failure were impossible. "He travels fastest who travels alone," applies not only cynically to the unwed, but to those who are not wed to thoughts and feelings of failure. Be single-minded. "If thine eye be single, thy whole body (being) shall be filled with light (inspiration)." Or, when you've put your hand to the plow don't look back.

Even the most inspired life has its moments of wavering, of uncertainty. Such a time is the time to "come to yourself," to review all the good things you know, to say with a friend of mine, "I cannot give up now. I have too much invested." Right. Keep on keeping on.

6. Active Faith

"Pour out." Your faith is your fortune. Not somebody else's faith. Yours. Practice it in small things, until it is stalwart enough to encompass what you think of as larger things. Gird yourself with incessant affirmatives. Turn to the book of Hebrews, eleventh chapter. In *The Living Bible* the first verse begins: "What is faith? It is the confident assurance that something we want is going to happen. It is the certainty that what we hope for is waiting for us, even though we cannot see it up ahead."

Even though you can only see a step ahead — which is the story of Everyman's life, pretty well — take that step, with confidence that as you take it another step will become clear, and so step by step you will come into the fulfillment of the good you seek, or even better than you seek. But not much that is desirable happens until you take the steps that cause it to appear.

This is very hard for the materially-minded man to understand. Remember the story of the farmer who wanted to withdraw his money from the bank, only to put it back when he saw that it was really there? Everybody wanted to go fishing following Jesus' injunction to Peter that he would find the coin for taxes in a fish's mouth. But they missed the point, as we do, if we are expecting that story to be taken literally. Although Jesus could work wonders, He was not a wonder-worker. He was a practical idealist with the accent on the practical. What, in effect, He was saying in that story was, "Yes, it is right for us to pay taxes to Rome, more right still to pay our tithe to God. You are a fisherman, Peter. Go down to the sea and catch fish; that's the way to obtain the tax money."

Today, would He not say, "Do the thing you do best, the best you can do it; that's the way your need will be supplied"?

7. Distribution

"Pay thy debt." They stood afar off, the ten, for well they knew that even their

154

shadow, should it fall across someone, was thought to be defiling. "Jesus, Master, have mercy on us!" they cried. He looked on them with compassion, and commended them to go to the Jewish priest and show him that they were healed. And they went. But one came back, a despised Samaritan, and gave thanks. "Were there not ten healed?" asked Jesus. "Where are the nine?"

How many good things are lost to us, I wonder, by our failure to appreciate and acknowledge them? Indeed, have we then really possessed them in the truest sense? Be a tenth man, the one who returns and gives thanks?

Gratitude is a debt to be paid, no less so than a promissory note.

When we are in trouble, often we are vociferous in our protestations of what we will do if only we are able to get out of the mess we are in. Too often, when we get out, the asseverations are forgotten. A rhyme whose source I cannot locate but whose meaning persists comes to mind: "When he was ill, the devil a saint would be. / When he got well, the devil a saint was he!''

What follows some time of stringency abated, some emergency met, some prayer answered, may be the most important part of the whole experience. There may be no financial transaction involved, yet the obligation to ''pay the debt'' still applies, in the sense that the debt to be paid is a debt owed to ourselves. We are not free of the obligation until we have learned from the experience. Then we can write across the whole transaction, ''Paid in full.''

Anybody may go through some particular kind of challenge once. But if he faces the same kind of problem repeatedly, we may feel justified in thinking he has ''attracted'' the repetitions, as if there is some lesson involved that has not been learned. This is, may we say, more common sense than superstition. For every effect in life there must be an antecedent cause. Trying to change effects without changing causes is at most an expedient. If we work with causes we can predict results.

8. Conservation

"Pay your debt, and set aside that which is full," is part of the ancient wisdom. "Save a little for a rainy day," is the gloomy adaptation, but "for investment or opportunity" is more comprehensive. The practical farmer knows this. He sells some of the yield of the harvest to pay his debts, reserving some of the finest grain for replanting, and lives off the rest.

Prepared For Prosperity

We don't just learn music just to repeat the scales or a language just to be able to parse a sentence or recite a vocabulary. We don't explore the laws of health or prosperity just for the sake of knowing about them, but rather for their pragmatic value — to enable us to live a fuller, freer life: like breathing out and breathing in, conforming without constraint. To conform to the law is to find the freedom of the law.

MEDITATION

I am now happily aware that most of my resources are in the Invisible. They are on deposit and available in the bank of infinite abundance. Knowing this I am not encumbered by the multitude of riches that are potentially mine. I call them forth in response to a conscious desire or need for them, much as I draw funds from an earthly bank or call to remembrance something learned and stored away in my own subconscious, from which I can call it forth on a moment's notice. God's universal bank knows no failure, no scarcity, no lack. In it are all that I have learned and earned; more than this, all God has freely given me; I call them forth by faith and by works that are the affirmation of faith.

11
The Law of the Magic Lamp

When I was a beggarly boy,
   And lived in a cellar damp,
I had not a friend nor a toy,
   But I had Aladdin's lamp.
James Russell Lowell

The Turning Point

In all human attainments, the turning point from seeming defeat and despair to overcoming and success comes when we take hope, when we resolutely face our challenges and opportunities, take account of where we are, center our attention on the talents, abilities, and resources which by the grace of God we have, and act on faith.

It is notable that in the seemingly miraculous accounts of human attainment in the Old and New

Testaments, simple everyday things, things that were right at hand, were made the basis of achievements that far outreached the expected.

Elisha called forth abundance to meet the widow's need by making use of the little oil that she had in the house.

Gideon's little band put to rout the great hosts of the Midianites by a surprise attack, when they broke the silence of the night with the blare of three hundred trumpets and the shouts of the trumpeters, and broke the darkness of the hillsides surrounding the sleeping enemy by the glare of three hundred torches.

David slew the giant of the Philistines with a smooth stone hurled from a sling.

Jacob won a deferred dowry from his wily father-in-law, Laban, by means of a few spotted willow branches casually tossed into the watering troughs where the sheep and goats and cattle came to drink.

Jesus broke and shared portions of the five loaves and two fishes to feed the five thousand. He drew forth money from the fish's mouth to pay the tax to Rome. He put clay on the blind man's eyelids, and told him to go wash in the pool of Siloam, and come, seeing. He freed the demoniac of the tormenting thoughts and feelings that possessed him by His calm word of faith and power.

In Legend Too

We have recalled the legend of Aladdin and the wonderful lamp. The genie did not appear simply because Aladdin wanted him to. In fact he discovered the lamp — and the genie — quite by accident. But when the youth rubbed the lamp to give it a polish and restore it to usefulness, the genie appeared. That is only a part of the story, as no doubt you know, but it's the part that makes a point, as useful in these matter-of-fact scientific days as in the ancient times when people believed in genies and magic bottles.

Miracles of the Commonplace

In this time of affluence and great scientific discovery and invention, to experience the miracles of the commonplace takes faith and discernment. Nobody wants to start at the bottom and work up. Everybody wants to start at the top, or as near what they consider to be the top as they can manage. So for anyone to be willing to prove himself, to start anywhere there is an opening, may be regarded as an almost servile and out-dated humility. Yet it is actually a modest degree of self-confidence. It is like saying, "No matter where you put me at the start, I'll be so conscientious, I'll work so diligently that I will prove valuable if not invaluable!"

Even today probably many persons would like to think they could evoke a genie by rubbing a magic lamp or uncorking a magic bottle. In effect actually they can.

The tellers of such tales of old may have been wiser than at first we think, for their stories are mostly true to principle if not to fact. In this one *the genie appeared in response to a human effort. He refused to come in response to a selfish greed.* The storyteller seems to be telling us that the practical attitude is often more productive than the miraculous. And from the practical point of view rubbing the lamp seems to mean putting to the best possible use the things and talents that we possess.

Rub your lamp!

In ways as unexpected as the appearance of a genie, and as commonplace as finding an old lamp, or the appearance of the postman, or opening a door, ways may open for the more abundant good to appear in your life.

They Rubbed Their Lamp!

There is a kind of genie, which we might fancifully describe as a "mini-genius," in everybody. He does not appear at command, but more often by invitation. Ideas and the power to execute them come from the same source. Sometimes creative ideas seem to come spontaneously. In most cases they come as the result of some activity that prepares the way, so to speak. To use a very dated metaphor, you have to prime the pump. You have to do something to get the ball rolling, or to start the flow. As a writer, sometimes I have had to prepare copy on very short notice, when I didn't seem to have an idea in my mind that seemed worth putting on paper. I have found that just waiting has not usually been enough, so I would put a sheet of paper in the typewriter and write the first thing that came into mind, whether or not it seemed pertinent to the matter at issue. Soon I would get into a flow of ideas, or they would get into me! I'd write as rapidly as possible, and eventually discard the "priming" material. Again, as a public speaker, often I have started off with a prepared outline, and find very soon that new and fresh (or at least fresher) ideas would come to mind, from outer space or inner space or super space. No matter; they came!

Emerson said: "We do not yet trust the unknown powers of thought. Whence came all these tools, inventions, books, laws, parties, kingdoms? Out of the invisible world, through a few brains. The arts and institutions of men are created out of thought. The powers that make the capitalist are metaphysical, the force of method and force of will makes trade, and builds towns." And again: "A man should learn to detect and watch that gleam of light that flashes across his mind from within, more than the lustre of the firmament of bards and sages."

To some persons inspiration seems to appear only in response to pressure. A star reporter tells how her boss called upon her to do a very difficult character series. She protested that there wasn't time enough. "Are you a reporter, or aren't you?" he challenged. She got the job done. Irving Berlin was a last-minute song writer. The story is told of him that sometimes the ink would not be dry on the orchestral score of his songs on opening night of a show.

To others it works in exactly the

opposite way. Ideas "come to them" best when they are in a relaxed state of thought and feeling, a kind of reverie in which the mind and emotions are given free reign to roam as they will; in which the person may idly speculate on whatever comes into mind. It is said of Einstein that his theory of relativity evolved from his allowing his mind to conjecture what might result if space were considered free from traditional beliefs. In so doing he evolved the concept of space-time.

In either case the "unknown powers of thought" are appealed to, and what may seem a very trivial incident leads to unforeseen achievements.

Discoveries

The art of printing, which has so greatly facilitated education, is said to have resulted from someone long ago carving a cameo-type design on newly cut wood. The carver wrapped the block in parchment to protect it from damage, and discovered that sap from the wood left an imprint of the design on the parchment. What would happen, he speculated, if letters of the alphabet could be so carved and placed side by side to form words? By doing this thousands of copies of a book could be produced, instead of being copied laboriously one at a time — and printing was born.

Of the producing of books there is no end. One that came about by accident was compiled by Elbert Hubbard. He began collecting items of prose and verse that he found to be inspiring. Having them printed by his Roycroft press was an afterthought. It became a best seller, and now after more than half a century it still brings inspiration to many readers.

Mack Carlow started out to help his teen-aged son deliver the heavy Sunday papers on his route one especially blustery day. He took their only conveyance, an ancient delivery truck, which seemed very appropriate for the occasion. Following financial reverses, the family of five was living in one of the rented trailers in a trailer park. Mack was out of work and jobs were scarce. He was surprised how quickly the delivery of the papers was accomplished, with him and his son working together. It gave him an idea. Maybe they could make arrangements to deliver papers daily on a broader scale, to a wider neighborhood. And that is what happened. In seeking to meet their own need and rendering a service, they were in effect invoking a genie!

Meanwhile the mother of the family was creating an attractive garden around their trailer, which attracted attention from every visitor to the park. Largely because of this, the owner asked her to take charge of rentals for him, and later, when he wanted to sell, she and her husband were able to buy it. The returns put the children through school and Mack and his wife are enjoying a comfortable retirement.

Like Mack Carlow, another man with a family to support found himself out of work, and reverted to a childhood fondness for whittling to take his thought off his troubles. He whittled out a set of toys for his children, who took them to school to show their friends. The other children wanted some, so he made sets for them, just for the love of doing it. A tourist visiting the family of one of these children came to see him one day, to see if he would make some for her to give her friends. She was surprised to find that he was making them only as a diversion. She recognized his talent, got him materials and paints to produce them in quantity, and persuaded him to devote his full time to the project. He started with the woodshed as his factory, and became a wealthy man. He rubbed his lamp!

Women's Lib?

A Beverly Hills matron accustomed to wealth found that when her husband became afflicted by an incapacitating illness, the hospital and medical bills decimated their fortune. What could she do to maintain their home? Through the years at holiday time she had surprised her wealthy friends by a gift that they could not buy, a handsome box of homemade candies prepared with plenty of butter and choice imported chocolate. So she had some handsome folders printed and mailed to the names in her address book, announcing that she was embarking on a commercial enterprise, taking orders for her very special candies. The enterprise outgrew the kitchen of her home. Eventually she was the proprietor of an exclusive shop. Her products were displayed and sold more often in beautiful trays and bowls than in the more ordinary cardboard boxes.

Another woman, the last member of an aristocratic but impoverished Southern family, tided over a time of financial stringency by making use of the only kind of manual work she had ever done, which was fine embroidery. She got the idea when she was invited to a tea in the parlors of a traditional hotel which dated back to the antebellum days. The expansive windows of the ancient rooms were adorned by the heavy gold-braided velvet drapes, augmented by elaborate lace curtains. She observed that both the draperies and curtains were in need of repair. The proprietor was a longtime friend. She sent for him and somewhat hesitantly called attention to their condition. He was apologetic about their appearance but could find no one who was able to do the needed restoration. Boldly she offered to do the work, and enlisted some of her elderly genteel friends to help. The proprietor was glad to compensate her.

The Challenge of Leisure

But such adventures of self-expression are as important for persons of affluence as for persons in need.

People work shorter hours than did those of a generation ago. The work week in most cases is five instead of six or seven days. It may soon be four instead of five. The work days themselves are shorter. There is more free time. How shall it be spent, and where? In a neighborhood tavern? Watching television there or at home? People with nothing to do can be more miserable than people who are overworked at uncongenial tasks, unless they find a hobby, an interest, a diversion that takes them out of themselves. And the time to do this is before we are aware of the need.

Poets Too Have Known

Often the poets are philosophers and seers. Shakespeare wrote, " 'Tis the mind that makes the body rich," and

> Who steals my purse steals trash;
>   'tis something, nothing;
> 'Twas mine,'tis his, and has been
>   slave to thousands.

Pope declared that

> Satan now is wiser than of yore,
> And tempts by making rich,
>   not making poor.

Ella Wheeler Wilcox makes the point graphically:

I gave a beggar from my
    little store
Of well-earned gold. He spent
    the shining ore
And came again and yet again,
Still cold and hungry as before.

I gave a thought, and through that
    thought of mine
He found himself, the man,
    supreme, divine,
Fed, clothed, and crowned with
    blessings manifold,
And now he begs no more.

MEDITATION

I am the lad with Aladdin's lamp, and I
am the genie and the lamp itself, for I am
an actor playing the leading role — and all
the parts — in my own life's drama. I am
protean in character. I play a role so that
I may learn from enacting it, calling forth

latent abilities of which I become aware only in the performance. Yet all the while, in the deepest depths and the greatest heights of my being, I know, though at times but dimly, that I am in all and of all, because I am a part of the All-in-All, one with the Creative Principle of Being. I have elected to play my present role in the drama of life, so that I may experience as fact a facet of my many-sided potential. I am more than any part I play, transiently a son of earth, eternally a son of God and heaven, reclaiming my lost heritage, the remembrance of who and what I am in entirety, in eternity.

12
The Right Idea About Money

I have often been penniless; I have never been poor,

Mike Todd

A State of Mind

If you were offered a million dollars, tax free, on condition that you would not spend it, would you accept the offer? You might, reflecting that even if you couldn't actually spend it, the fact of possessing it would place you in an advantageous bargaining position, somewhat like the prospective heir to a fortune. But having no control over the sum, could it truthfully be said that you possessed it? And even if the condition were removed and you were granted the million outright, would you want the responsibilities of such possessions?

"I don't want to be a millionaire, I just want to live like one!" a friend of mine exclaims.

"What do you mean by that — to live like a millionaire?" I countered.

"Why, never to have to worry about money again," he said.

That, I think, is quite an assumption. I one time travelled with a group of friends on a trip to Florida, among whom was a sure-enough millionaire. As I came down to the lobby of the hotel one morning to join the others at breakfast, I was startled to see our millionaire pacing the floor with what looked like a telegram in one hand, the other hand mopping his brow.

"Oh Ben! What has happened?" I exclaimed, thinking that someone dear to him must have met with an accident or a fatality.

To my amazement it was neither. A complicated financial deal had been consummated — successfully — but it meant that he would be losing a couple of day's interest on the sum involved before it could be reinvested! This was the cause of his distress! By which I realized that there is more to being a millionaire than appears to less affluent people.

End vs. Means

Surely money is not to be considered an end in itself but only a sometimes precarious means to an end. *Too much of it — that is more than we know how to handle — can be a plague, just as too little — less than what we need — can be a famine.*

Paul's allusion to money has been generally misquoted as "money is the root of all evil," whereas what he really wrote in his first letter to Timothy (6:10) is: "The love of money is the root of all evil: which while some coveted after, they have erred from the faith, and pierced themselves through with many sorrows." *The Living Bible* gives a version that is hardly recognizable at first reading, but much easier to understand, rendering the passage: "Do you want to be truly rich? You already are if you are happy and good. After all, we didn't bring any money with us when we came into the world, and we can't carry away a single penny when we die.'' (Dr. Kenneth N. Taylor who produced this version of Scripture says that it is a thought-by-thought translation instead of word for word, more accurate because Hebrew and Greek are so different from English in their approach.)

You are rich if you are happy and good!

Be happy. Be good. The formula is as simple and as difficult as that, compressed into just four little words, but so challenging to achieve that a whole lifetime does not seem enough in which clearly to discern and to express, in a world of relative values, these qualities which all the world is seeking.

Where and how shall we find answers that bring a sense of contentment and well-being?

Many of us have been reared in forms of religious faith that make it appear that almost everything the heart desires is either ''illegal, immoral, or fattening'';

as if the Creative Principle of Being had given us the desire for health, happiness, well-being, prosperity, and at the same time had said in effect, "Oh, you'd like to have all those things, would you? Well, you cannot. You must sin and suffer and be miserable, die in the forlorn hope that in an afterlife you may be one of the favored few who will be provided with all that you have lacked in the present life, and not cast into the outer darkness," which an ancient theology warns us is to be the fate of many. This would seem more like a plan of a demon than the Deity.

There is a legend about a king of olden times who had, it would seem, all the riches that this world could give, yet could find no happiness in them. He sought the counsel of a saintly sage who admonished him, "Go out into the highways and byways and search for a happy man. Get from him his shirt and coat, and in wearing them you will find happiness." He searched his realm until he found such a man, but alas, that man had neither shirt nor cloak.

Superficially then we are to assume that the king would be happier if he discarded his own shirt and cloak. Actually, of course, there is no one area or condition of life that is the guarantee of happiness, for happiness is an inside job, and we are about as happy as we allow ourselves to be.

A By-product

Apparently most people are not very permissive in this regard. They allow themselves to be anything but happy. With whom, among the many persons that you know, would you be willing to exchange places? Would you want to be like? And of all the people you know well, who would you say are the happiest?

Without exception, do they not appear to be those who lose themselves in some interest, hobby, concern, or service that takes them, as we say (wrongly perhaps), "out of themselves"?

Among them you might find a garage mechanic who prides himself on using his skill to turn out a good job, a sculptor who in agony and ecstasy reveals the angel in the stone, the father who guides his little son's first steps.

It may be persons like Dr. Louis Leakey and his wife who for decades devoted themselves to a search for the site of man's first appearance on earth, and in the Olduvai gorge of East Africa came upon the vestigial remains of early man dating back some two million years.

It may be a dedicated youth who devotes his energies to helping underprivileged and handicapped children find greater fulfillment. It may be a comedian who escapes from the sense of his own limitation into a world of imagery into which by his skill he transports his audience.

The great Galilean summed it up in a sentence: "He that findeth his life shall lose it; and he that loseth his life for my sake shall find it." In today's terminology this seems to mean that he who is too wrapped up in himself ("findeth his life") may exist but doesn't really live, while he who loses himself in some unselfish and creative purpose ("for my sake") finds his higher, liberated self. As an octogenarian friend of mine put it in part, "The man who is all wrapped up in himself makes a very small bundle." And happiness is the by-product of a way of life.

Back to Paul Again

Let's turn again to Paul's first letter to Timothy, chapter six, the seventeenth and eighteenth verses: "Tell those who are rich not to be proud and not to trust in their money, which will soon be gone, but their pride and trust should be in the living God who always richly gives us all we need for our enjoyment. Tell them to use their money to do good. They should be rich in good works and should give happily to those in need" *(The Living Bible)*.

Paul shared a related thought with the Corinthians when he said, in effect, "Everyone must make up his own mind how much he should give. Don't force anyone to give more than he really wants to, for cheerful givers are the ones God prizes'' (II Corinthians 9:7).

Jesus made much the same point when a wealthy young man approached Him and asked what he must do to attain to eternal life. Jesus replied that he must keep the commandments, and named over several of them.

''I've always obeyed every one of them,'' the youth responded. ''What else must I do?''

''Go and sell everything you have and give the money to the poor, and then come follow me,'' said Jesus, and looking on him loved him.

But the youth went away sadly, for he was very rich.

Turning to the little group of disciples around Him, Jesus commented, ''How hard it is for those who trust in riches to enter the kingdom of God. . . . It is easier for a camel (or a rope) to go through the eye of a needle than for a rich man to enter the kingdom.''

We are coming close to the right idea about money in the light of these comments, for *we never really attain to the right idea about money until we overcome the fear of being without it.*

"More Stately Mansions"

Thomas Edison knew this. He knew that rich ideas are the only real wealth. He believed that ideas came to him "from the blue," or, as you might say, from super space or a higher mind. His life is the empirical evidence for this, because since the time of Leonardo da Vinci no one has brought forth so many inventive ideas to bless the world. He knew this so well that when, at the height of his career, his Orange, New Jersey, laboratories and workshop caught fire in the night and were rapidly reduced to ruin, he was undismayed.

An aide hastened to the inventor's bedside, wakening him from sleep, and shouted the tragic news into his deaf ears.

"Do what you can and then go back to bed. We'll build some new ones in the morning!" he declared.

Build them of course he did, for he knew the truth about riches; that money and other possessions are only symbols of true riches. *Ideas are coin of the mind realm.* Neither moths nor rust consume them, nor can thieves break in and steal. And ideas can be shaped and fashioned in any form that the creative mind of man can conceive. So a man is rich or poor primarily not in proportion to his material possessions, but in his freedom from and mastery of them, his faith in his ability to call them forth when they are needed, or replace them when they are expended.

A Very Ancient Problem

It is a very ancient problem, the tendency to mistake the symbol for the reality that it represents. Money is not actually wealth, but only a convenient symbol, a medium of exchange. We don't have to be spiritually illuminated to find confirmation for this notion. The evidence is signalled to us on every hand.

A bird builds its nest in the branches of a slender tree growing by a waterfall. The wind sways the tree trunk, sways the branches even more, tosses the nest about, drenches it with spray. But the bird is not dismayed. Its security is not in the tree trunk, or the branches, or even in the nest, but in its wings!

A man who had twice been a millionaire sought spiritual counsel just after he had lost his second fortune in a market crash. He pulled his pants' pockets wrong side out to show how empty they were. "I hardly have a dollar to my name!" he confessed.

"You have lost a great deal," the counselor responded.

"Young man, I want you to know I haven't lost anything. I am more capable now than I have ever been. I have a wife and three daughters who love me and have faith in me. I am going out and make another million," he declared. He was evidently a better producer than steward, but he had the right grasp on principle!

An Honest Deception

In what would to most people seem to be a deception, a friend of mine demonstrated his faith in this principle. He had very little money but a big idea. He needed extensive office space in which to present what he had to offer. "A great idea deserved an impressive setting," he reasoned, so he rejected the cheaper storefronts in the poorer sections of the city. His heart was set on one of the finest locations in the best part of town.

"You haven't a chance of getting it," his wife said. "The owner will demand an advance payment, references, and a guarantee!"

"Wait and see," he replied calmly. "I believe I will get it."

To her surprise he returned in due time with the good news that his application was accepted.

"When they asked about my financial background, I just smiled and said, 'I have a rich father!' "

"Wasn't that an out-and-out deception?" she asked. "Didn't the owner demand more assurance that you could pay the rent?''

''No, it wasn't a deception. I do have a rich Father, with a capital F, and I have faith in Him, faith in myself, faith in the product I shall be offering. Whether or not the owner recognized that capital F, he didn't say. All he did say was, ''I like your spirit. Move in whenever you are ready!''

This is a true story, an almost unbelievable one except to someone who has discovered that truth is indeed often stranger than fiction. I am glad to report that both the owner's and my friend's faith were justified. The project was a success, and the owner got his rent on time.

''Would you recommend such a procedure?'' some reader would surely ask if he had the opportunity.

No, I would not. It would not work out, and should not, unless the assertion was an honest one. And how often would you find a wealthy owner of select business property who would accept an ''unsupported'' statement, ''I have a rich Father''? It would have to be by what I call "divine appointment." But it did happen, and I add it to a long list of "unsupportable" true experiences that have happened to people I know, and to me. I am reminded of a letter I had from a correspondent whom I've never seen, but who had written me for help during a very challenging time of being without adequate funds and without work. The report of a good outcome was summarized in the closing statement of his letter: "God opens ways where to human sense there seems to be no way."

Like but Unlike

Trying to fit your own sense of need, your own level of awareness, to details of the manner in which things have worked out for somebody else is like trying to match two leaves on a tree. No two instances are ever identical. But the principle back of them all is the same. The way they work out has to be compatible to the consciousness of the personalities involved.

"In a drawer of my sewing machine I keep all kinds of buttons from discarded garments," an octogenarian acquaintance comments. "I always find a use for them sometime. They come in various sizes, shapes, and colors. When you need a certain kind to match a missing one you may have to hunt for awhile until you find the right one. People are like that. You get the right one in the right place to do what needs to be done, and it's just wonderful!" And I most heartily agree.

I bargained with Life for a penny,
    And Life would pay no more,
However, I begged at evening
    When I counted my scanty store.

For Life is a just employer,
    He gives you what you ask;
But once you have set the wages,
    Why, you must bear the task.

I worked for a menial's hire,
    Only to learn, dismayed,

That any wage I had asked of Life,
Life would have paid.

Jessie Rittenhouse

MEDITATION

I picture a sheet of music before me. It is not really music itself, but only the notation of music that can be transformed into glorious melodic sound beneath the fingers of the skilled musician. I picture money in a comparable way; it is not of itself wealth, and it represents services rendered, products produced, and it can be redeemed in terms of food, shelter, clothing, and recreation.

I do not denigrate or depreciate money. I am grateful for it and for what it symbolizes. I bless all the money that I receive, all that I have, and all that I pass on to others. I bless all my transactions that involve the use of money, to the service of mankind.

13
The Secret Way of Abundance

When things are tight, something — or somebody — has to give.

Where's the Money Coming From?

"Sure, it's a good idea, but where is the money coming from to carry it out?"

Familiar words. How often we've heard them, maybe even said them! Through the years I have often heard them from businessmen, most often from executive board members with whom I have worked, businessmen mostly, who should know better than anybody what is the real truth about such matters; which is, that the means to carry out a good idea do not come of themselves, but in response to ideas which can spark the imagination and vision, and initiative that will inspire faith.

Many of us are still like the farmer we've already mentioned, who went to the bank and announced that he wanted to withdraw the money in his account. The teller complied, and placed the pile of currency on the window shelf. "OK. Now you can put it back. I just wanted to be sure it was there!"

Most progress has to be initiated when the supply is not obvious, or at least not active, which is probably why Paul said that "faith is the substance of things hoped for, the evidence of things not seen."

Money Doesn't "Come"

A church which had been built during World War II cost more than was anticipated. Local funds were exhausted long before it was completed. Then someone had the bright idea of reaching beyond the local membership and inviting people at a distance to contribute the cost of a brick toward its construction. The notion appealed to a large number of people (who in some instances visited the church and wanted to see which particular brick they had paid for!). Stained glass for windows in the areas of worship was not available, and a simulation of stained glass was used in some areas. For twenty-five years the windows in most of the edifice remained virtually colorless. Finally someone said, "We should have some beautiful windows further to represent the beauty of the faith that the church represents."

"We don't have the money. It will cost too much. Where is the money coming from?" were objections that were raised.

"Let's see if we can get some small simulated models made, and determine how people will respond to the idea," was suggested.

The models were made, announcement of the plan was presented, members of the congregation were offered the opportunity of contributing the cost of a window to be installed as a memorial to some friend or loved one. Within a few months all the windows were subscribed and paid for. The regular income of the church did not suffer, in fact it increased somewhat. The interest and participation of hundreds of members was stimulated.

Money does not ''come'' from somewhere unless someone brings it. It is intended to circulate, to be used. Good circulation promotes good financial health, as good circulation in the human organism promotes good physical health.

A dollar bill put in the sugar bowl or somebody's sock remains just a dollar. Invested it will yield a certain amount of interest, which is like rent being paid for its use. Passed from one person to another to pay for some service or commodity, the same dollar bill may pass through an incalculable number of hands, and with it or its equivalent return to the person who first put it into circulation.

You Have to Believe

One thing we find in common in all human overcomings and attainments: in the dark clouds of doubt, fear, and despair there appears a tiny spark of hope. It may be no more than a vagrant, passing thought, more a feeling than a thought. It takes the form of such words as "maybe," "perhaps," "just possibly," but it is the turning point.

Maybe, perhaps, and possibly are not strong enough to sway men's minds, or to promote large enterprises; but they are a beginning, like the faltering steps of a youngster learning to walk. They are strong words in the sense that t. 'y are at least a beginning, a turning point from inaction to action. Nothing happens until we initiate action.

"Ideas are coin of the mind realm." But ideas must be put into activity just as currency must circulate. "Hard times" are another term for inaction or lack of faith. When things are tight, something has to give. When times are tight, *somebody* (everybody) has to give!

As long as we say, "It is impossible," or "I don't see how it can be done," we are closing the door against betterment. Someone has to see at least a possibility, and think a little farther, take at least a step. Many an enterprise that required many steps began when even the first step was taken on faith.

The Secret Way

There is a secret way of abundance; it is available to everyone, but not everyone finds it, and even some of those who have found it do not realize the secret.

The ancient Hindus knew it.

The Hebrews knew it.

Jesus knew it most of all.

The Master referred to it when he said, "Is it not written in your law, I said, Ye are gods?" and again, "The Son of man is come to save that which was lost."

The Hindus have a legend that at one time all men were gods, but because they abused their power, Brahma hid it where men would seek and find it last,

197

within themselves.

Paul the apostle put it, "Know ye not that ye are the temple of God, and that the spirit of God dwelleth in you?"

Angela Morgan wrote:

I am aware of the splendor that ties
All of the things of the earth
   with the things of the skies.

Emerson wrote:

I am the owner of the sphere,
   Of the seven stars and the solar year,
Of Caesar's hand, and Plato's brain,
   Of Lord Christ's heart, and
     Shakespeare's strain.

Teilhard de Chardin wrote, "— lay on me fully both by the Within and the Without of myself, grant that I may never break this double thread of my life."

That man should find again that which was lost, a sense of his own innate oneness with his Creator, and through it learn the secret way to abundance of all good things, is the awareness that can bring man into a new age of health, bounty, peace, well-being.

Truly, every good desire of the heart shall be fulfilled, either in ways that we now see, or in ways that in God's sight are even better. This does not come about by chance or magic but by law — universal law; for this is an orderly universe, and order is heaven's first law. It is the first law of this earth plane, too.

Reconciliation

This is the great reconciliation that can be tranforming in its effect; that though transiently and in appearance we are sons of earth, eternally we are sons of God and heaven. Thus, as Paul implied, our two natures are reconciled in one body. We are to bring together what has become separated.

Equivalence

Our first step is to become strong in the realization that nature's first law is the Law of Equivalence, of sowing and reaping, cause and effect, action and reaction. You cannot do wrong and feel right. Sow the wind, and you reap the whirlwind. But by the same token, no good effort is lost. Everything brings forth after its kind.

Begin at the beginning; in thought, feeling, word, and carry these over to right action. "First the blade, then the ear, then the full grain in the ear." Everything works from within out. You cannot even raise your arm without the thought of doing it.

Patterns

Our life tends always to out-picture the character of the inner life, its habitual thoughts, moods, feelings. Change these and you change the outward form of your life. If you don't like what appears, change the inner patterns that it expresses. Motion pictures illustrate the concept. If you don't like the pictures that appear on the screen, your major concern is not with the screen but with the film. Change the film and you change the picture.

Be Aware

Even people who readily grasp this concept are still only vaguely aware of what they actually do think, feel, and say. There is the human tendency to resist discipline, or even to be unaware of the need of it. We tend to excuse bad habits of the inner life as we excuse social errors with the comment, "of course I know better, but —!" Which is reminiscent of the allegory about the wealthy matron who died and went to heaven. She was met by St. Peter or someone who represented him. She demanded to be taken to her heavenly home.

"Come with me, madam," he responded, and led the way down a

handsome avenue lined with lovely homes. As they proceeded, the avenue became narrower, the houses more modest. Finally they were walking down a dirt road, and came to an unsightly hovel.

"This is your abode," he said.

"What do you mean!" the woman exclaimed indignantly.

"We did the best we could with what you sent ahead," he replied.

Predictable, Not Magical

The secret way of abundance is not a magical way of effortless achievement. It requires discipline, not that life is a hard master, or that God wants to make things hard for us, but because we have dwelt so exclusively on the materialistic way of life that life is out of balance.

We have to renew our remembrance of who and what we are, not to reject or condemn the world in which we live, but to correct our concept of our relationship to it. This becomes easier with practice, until, as we say, "it becomes second nature" and really represents a return to our "first" nature.

A New Vocabulary

Build a "Spiritual Vocabulary." Feed your soul on nourishing food as persistently and regularly as you feed your body. Seek out books, poems, plays, and places that give you inspiration. Read the Psalms, the Gospels, and Epistles in the Bible. Read Emerson's "Self-Reliance," "Compensation," "The Oversoul." Follow Elbert Hubbard's hobby and make a scrapbook of your own. Jot down some affirmative soul-builders on the order of the following:

I am a child of the living God. I have within me the power to express my best self.

The power of God within me is mightier than anything that afflicts or affrights me from within or without.

I am adequate and more than

adequate for whatever I am called upon to meet.

God in the midst of me is mighty.

"The Lord is my shepherd; I shall not want."

Dr. Frank Crane once wrote about what he thought were the sins of the churches. The chief one was that salvation is free. In a sense he is right, if by that he meant that we cannot buy our way "into the kingdom." But money is not the only price we pay; and there is a price on everything; the price of interest, attention, evaluation, responsiveness, among others. Although we are surrounded by a relatively unlimited atmosphere, we cannot get another breath until we give the one we have.

In a world where there is a monetary price on almost everything, giving with no thought of return could well become a lost art unless we really work at it, yet it is the most effective and perhaps the only really true form of giving. For we are making patterns by our way of life, our attitudes. Give as you would receive; richly, freely, promptly.

Radiate

Brown Landone reminded us that the kingdom of heaven actually signifies the realm of expansion; that the word "heaven" means expanded (heave; an upward motion; a rising). In a mental-emotional sense we might take this to mean radiate. So if we can accept the Scriptural statements that the kingdom of heaven is at hand and the kingdom of God is within us, then we come again to the thought that creativity is basically an inward thing; something that is an upward movement, a rising, a radiation that begins within ourselves.

"If you want to be strong, act as if you are strong; if you want to be happy, act as if you are happy," someone has said. So by the same token, if you want to experience more of the well-being that heaven implies, dare to affirm, *"I am a radiant center of Christ light, mighty to attract my good, and to radiate good to others.''* ("The reach must oft exceed the grasp, else what were heaven for!")

What we send out, or radiate, always tends to come back. That is an important step on the secret way of abundance — enough to work at for a long and very rewarding time.

Dare, Share, Prepare

Dare to put your faith to the test of experience; do so even if you feel that you don't have very much faith. You have to plant the idea of faith in the fertile ground of imagination in order for it to grow. Sharing your good ideas, your good spirits, your appreciation, your time, and your talents with others is like making deposits in a bank. They draw interest in both meanings of the word, and they will increase to your blessing and that of others as you apply yourself to these concepts.

Of course anything you do because you enjoy doing it, find it interesting, is more effective than if you do it because you are practicing an unfamiliar rule and role. What you strongly think and deeply feel is more effective in practical living; and deep feeling is more effective than thinking. The ideal is a combination of both. Even a sporadic application of these concepts helps. It helps most when it becomes habitual, when it becomes a way of life. Conforming to this pattern is like making deposits in a bank that never fails. You can call on your spiritual resources in every need; a very present help and resource.

MEDITATION

Conscious of my oneness with God, who is my ever-present, unfailing richness and support, I am freed from all sense of limitation, all fear of lack. I rest my affairs securely in the open, bountiful hand of God. I am established in the realization of my innate ability to manifest the wisdom, efficiency, and foresight which will make me a channel of abundant supply. I call upon the powers that God has given me, knowing that as I develop the ability to give my services, my love, and myself, efficiently and helpfully, I shall attract abundant recompense. I live within the very shadow of the Almighty, sheltered by the God who is above all gods that men bow down and worship. He alone is my refuge and resource, my very present help. From the center of life and light within me, I radiate love and good will, bounty and blessing to all.

14
Beyond the End of Things

Behold, I have set before thee an open
door, and no man can shut it.

Revelation 3:8

Three Things You Can Do

When you are "at the end of your rope,"
there are three things you can do. You can
let go, you can tie a knot in the rope and
hang on, or you can splice the rope and
begin again. None of these notions is
original and only one of them is worth
serious consideration. The first is
destructive, the second is negative, and
only the third is constructive.

There is a time in most people's lives
when, if they are looking at things past,
they see a door closed or closing. They

need to change their outlook, realize that there is more truth than poetry in the old bromide that "no door closes but another opens." This has pretty good Scriptural authority too, for we find the Revelator asserting, "Behold, I have set before thee an open door, and no man can shut it."

If we look beyond the end of anything, we shall find a fresh beginning. But the trouble with many of us is that when we reach what seems to be "the end of things," we are unprepared for it. (We have seen the same thing or something similar happening to others but somehow it usually seems like something that will never happen to us.) We may become so confused or so overcome by pain or grief or discouragement that we fail to look further along. Or looking through misty eyes we do not see, or seeing do not understand.

Jesus recognized this very human trait when He said, "I have yet many things to say unto you, but you cannot bear them now," or, in effect, "There is a lot that I want to share with you, but it is beyond your present understanding."

Growth is a law of life, and grow we must, into mental and emotional, as well as physical, maturity. It doesn't always come about easily. Some accomplish this with relative ease, others only with stress and strain. To the latter, by way of consolation, it might be said that this plane of life is a far from perfect world in which to have everybody and everything agree with us, catering to our whims and moods; but it is a well-nigh perfect world in which to learn and grow, to call forth "the imprisoned splendor within us."

Calf-Consciousness

Florence Crawford described the people who can only grow through stress and strain as having "calf-consciousness," and illustrated the point by what happened in a wealthy family of her acquaintance. They had a ten-year-old boy for whom they wanted to get a birthday present. He already had everything a boy might like that they could think of. Finally they did the ultimate obvious thing. They asked him what he would like to have.

He thought a long time. He had a bat and glove, innumerable toys, a bicycle, a pony. Finally he came up with a novel idea. "I'd like to have a calf!" he declared.

"Oh yes, a calf," they murmured. But how does one go about getting a calf? Came a brilliant idea! "We'll go to the stockyards!" they exclaimed. So they went in their chauffeur-driven limousine to get a calf and transport him to pastures green where, to coin a phrase, he might lead a bully life.

Did the little animal appreciate being saved from an early demise? Indeed he did not. It took several men to lift and tug and push and pull him into the tonneau of the car, struggling against them, bawling all the way to the country estate of his rescuers.

"Many people," said Mrs. Crawford, "have calf-consciousness. They fight every step of the way that will lead them to something better than their present perceptions invite."

A Measure of Perception

"It is one of the commonest of mistakes to consider that the limit of our power of perception is also the limit of all there is to perceive," declares C. W. Leadbeater. So that what is impossible to a person in one level of awareness may well be possible to a person of more extended awareness.

The ministry of Jesus is replete with incidents that illustrate this fact. There was a youth grievously tormented by an affliction that seemed incurable to the multitude, and most especially to the father of the afflicted youth, who appealed to Jesus for help. Jesus said to him, "If thou canst believe, all things are possible to him that believeth." And the father cried out with tears, "Lord, I believe; help thou mine unbelief." And the youth was restored to health.

If the affliction had seemed as incurable to Jesus as to the multitude, no healing would have occurred.

Everything is real to its corresponding level of perception, but it is like only a shadow of reality to a higher level of perception. An intimation of this challenging concept can be found close at hand. For instance, hold your hand in such a manner that its shadow is cast on a flat surface. To what philosophers call Flatland, a theoretical realm of two dimensions, like the surface of the plane on which the shadow appears, it could be real, but it is only a shadow of the hand as it appears in our level of perception.

"Only believe. All things are possible to him who believes." There is great truth in this admonition. There are also fallacies in what we take the words to mean. Faith does not make true something that is not true; it might make the untruth seem true to the believer. What faith *can* do is to reveal to the believer a truth that had been unrecognized previously. It is seeing something from a higher viewpoint, and by sustaining the higher perception, attaining freedom from the limitations of a lower one.

Some things are too hard for most

people to believe. People are like the woman who said, "I can believe everything in the Gospels except the precious promises!" But even though some of what are called the miracles are too much for our habitual level of awareness and response, most of us have at least fleeting moments of transcendent awareness of another level of consciousness in which the so-called miracles that occasionally occur in this world are accepted as the natural order of being; a realm in which there is no more death, neither sorrow nor crying, neither any more pain, for these "former things" have been done away, and all is made new. Sadly we relegate such concepts to an afterlife, whereas Jesus, and to some degree others, have not only believed these things to be possible in this present three-dimensional world, but have proved them in sufficient ways and times and places to warrant faith that they are not idle dreams, but intimations of the higher potential of which all mankind is capable.

"But I'm not Jesus Christ," perhaps you say. And of course none of us is. But

He was not joking when He assured us that we could be more like Him, overcoming present limitations, attaining to greater things.

Maybe the fact that we can never be quite content with failure is an intimation that there is more of His nature in us all than we have generally recognized; that as one has said, we were "born not to defeat but to victory." That innate conviction has brought many a person out of what seemed to be the end of things into new life and attainment.

A woman who tragically lost an only child made her grief a monument to him by mothering many children reared in institutions where the personal affection and security that are the right of every child are hard to come by.

A man who had twice made and lost a fortune, set out in middle age to make a third.

An aging opera star, who had long dominated the opera field, frankly recognized the changes in her voice that came with years and in her maturity made a new career as a *lieder* singer. A man who lost his voice to cancer mastered esophageal speech and not only taught it to other laryngectomees, but taught a church choir as well.

Overcomers

Often I think of the young woman whose potential screen career was blighted by an unfortunate accident that marred her physical beauty. Courageously she went on to earn a living writing for screen magazines, and wrote a popular song and a successful play despite a series of heartaches and misfortunes.

"Gertrude, you've gone through a lot!" I sympathized.

"Doctor Wilson, I want you to know I've *come* through a lot!" she responded; and looking at her proud posture, her smiling face and sparkling eyes, I could agree. And I think often of the difference between *going* through something and coming *through* it!

Call the roll of people you know about, the overcomers who have discovered their P.A. (for personal adequacy) as Lloyd C. Douglas, a pretty fair overcomer himself, called it. You might start with Steinmetz, seldom free from physical pain, yet rising above it to contribute so much to the world's electrical progress; Beethoven and Edison who surmounted deafness; the two distantly related Roosevelts, one who became a Rough Rider, the other a kind of benevolent overrider; and George Washington Carver, whose prayerful dedication to the South in which he was born helped so greatly to free it from the economic limitations of dependency upon a single and sometimes temperamental product, the cotton crop.

And Remember

They were geniuses, you say? They may well have been; or it could be that they just refused to accept the limitations of the degree of perception generally shared by others, and dared to question them and consider what might be the result if one (or more) of these limitations could be transcended. So indeed might you or I or anyone, at least to the point of changing and even transforming our own life and world. We can adjust. We can expand our horizon. And the wider that horizon becomes, the greater will be our faith in the transcendent wisdom, love, beauty, and purpose of the Creative Principle in whose infinite life our life is immerged.

Adapt, Adjust, Agree

We cannot change the fundamental laws of the universe, and if we could it would undoubtedly be for the worse instead of for the better. But we can adjust. We can adapt. We can agree. And if we work *with* these laws they will work *for* us. Most of us probably accept this belief in general, and as we observe them to apply to others. Most of us need to adjust to it *in the particulars* of personal challenge.

No one welcomes pain, yet surely it is nature's way of telling us that something is out of order and needs to be corrected.

We no longer consider it to be the personal punishment of a vindictive deity; rather a beneficent, but very definite, warning of some condition that has an unknown or unheeded cause.

Most of us would like to prolong indefinitely some relationship or condition that we find pleasant, but actually due for change. My mother and maybe yours was like this.

Coming home from one of my first days at school, I found her seated in her bedroom with an open trinket-box on her lap, viewing with tear-stained eyes a baby's outgrown shoes, a preschool lock of hair. Did she then wish me always to be the infant who had outgrown the shoe, the growing boy who had discarded curls? Did she not want me to grow up? Would she not have wept more, and with more reason, had I remained forever the babe she could nestle in her arms, the toddler with the auburn curls?

Midstream

We dwell for a time between two vast eternities, the mysterious realm of the past from which we have come at birth and the future into which we disappear at death. Whatever our individual belief about these two experiences may be, it is very difficult and not very mature to ignore them, or to try to have the one without the other. The testimony of their relationship is everywhere evident about us. Even within us. When Paul said, centuries ago, "I die daily" and "the body, though it be one, has many members," he was stating what we now call a scientific truth; for the body is indeed composed of myriad tiny bodies, living their little life-spans, having their births and deaths and replacements.

If you can entertain the concept that life is a continuum; that birth and death are events in the midst of life; that it is not life and death that are opposites, but birth and death — two ways of viewing that same experience — you are well on the way to overcoming the last enemy.

Looking back we see death, looking forward we see birth, but life surrounds them both, forever changing, but forever be-ing.

The Enduring Bond

This is to some of us a comforting philosophy, again perhaps easy to accept in the universal sense, more challenging to accept in the particular.

I think of a lovely white-haired woman who had comforted probably hundreds of persons facing the challenge of bereavement. Then her aged and physically infirm husband made what she called "the transition." He had been ill a long time, his body was grievously afflicted. Although mentally she accepted this as offering freedom from the garment of flesh that no longer served him well, she was emotionally inconsolable. She "wore her grief like a monument." Her friends tried to be comforting and consoling, but ended up in exhaustion. Finally one day several of us were riding somewhere together. She was a member of the group, casting a cloud of gloom over the occasion. Finally a man about her own age resorted to desperate measures — the shock treatment. "What do you want to do, Charlotte, have God arrested because your husband died?" She looked at him as if she was about to slap him. ("I wouldn't have blamed her if she did," he confesses.) Then her face cleared in a smile. "That is kind of ridiculous of me, isn't it!" she exclaimed. "Well, yes, for a person with your spiritual insight," he responded.

It isn't only what we know or believe, but what we do about it that really counts.

Death is not a wall but a door. It is birth to another realm of life, viewed from the underside.

And since we've come this far in thinking about it, perhaps we can consider another possible step. Shall we find again those who have gone through that door?

There are some human associations that are naturally transient. They serve a special place in our life, and when the purpose is served the association naturally ends. Not all the same persons occupy a large place in our life today that did so ten or twenty years ago. There are some associations that are so compelling that they last as long as both members are in this plane of life. But there are some such bonds that are so strong and deep, so much of the spirit and so little of the flesh, that not even the change called death contrives against them. Such souls seem ever near. So near that sometimes we seem to hear the well-loved voice, see the well-remembered face, and find thereby a great and immortal possession that nothing can take away.

The Voyager

"I am standing upon the seashore. A ship at my side spreads her white sails to the morning breeze and starts for the blue ocean. She is an object of beauty and strength and I stand and watch her until at length she hangs like a speck of white cloud just where the sea and sky come to mingle with each other.

"Then someone at my side says, 'There! She's gone!' Gone where? Gone from my sight, that is all. She is just as large in mast and hull and spar as she was when she left my side, and she is just as able to bear her load of living weight to her destined port.

"Her diminished size is in me, not in her. And just at the moment when someone at my side says, 'There! She's gone,' there are other eyes watching her coming, and other voices ready to take up the glad shout, 'There she comes!' And that is dying." — *Anon.*

MEDITATION

I live in the great forever, and am immersed in the ocean of truth. As my level of awareness and response rises I become increasingly aware of my true nature as a child of the Most High. My troubles are dispelled, not by denying them, but by surmounting them. There shall be lamps for my darkness, the oil of gladness for my tears of sorrow. I find myself enwrapped in God's everlasting arms of love; they support and sustain me. With healing He heals me, and I am made whole. I wear the sandals of understanding, the robe of righteousness; the crown of attainment rests lightly upon my brow. I am still in the world, but I am no longer overwhelmed by its powers and principalities. I yield to them, work with them, conform to them, but no longer fearfully or abjectly, because I am reaching past the sense of becoming into the sense of Being.

The publishers hope that this Large Print Book has brought you pleasurable reading. Each title is designed to make the text as easy to see as possible. If you wish a complete list of the Large Print Books we have published, ask at your local library or write directly to:

G. K. Hall & Co.
70 Lincoln St.
Boston, Mass. 02111